Chess

for

Beginners

Chess

for

Beginners

by

D B Pritchard

Typeset in 11pt Times New Roman by Letterpart Ltd., Reigate, Surrey.

Printed and bound in Great Britain by Cox & Wyman Ltd., Reading, Berkshire.

Clarion: published from behind no. 80 Brighton Road, Tadworth, Surrey, England. For information about our company and the other books we publish, visit our website at www.clarion-books.co.uk

Contents

Foreword

Many diagrams in this book show only a section of the chessboard to save space. Where the section includes a corner or edge of the board this is clearly illustrated, *but in every case the whole of the chessboard is in use, with the exception of the constructional problems in Part One.*

Cross-references are freely used: for example, (**59***B*) refers to diagram *B* in section **59**. An Index is also given at the end.

A chess set is needed to follow the latter part of the book. The standard 'Staunton pattern' men are recommended.

Introduction

Chess is very old. Its descent can be traced directly from the game of chaturanga, played in India thirteen centuries ago and probably much before that. In these early times, dice were often used to determine the man to be moved.

From India, the game spread the way things did in those days – along trade routes and in the wake of armies. In these historical movements the game underwent changes so that today we find (for example) Chinese and Japanese chess (respectively xiangqi and shogi) – both developed from the early game – played very differently from our chess.

The game moved west from India, through Persia to the Moslem lands, and into Western Europe by way of Spain and Italy in about the 9th century, but it was not until some six hundred years later that it was played in its present form.

Throughout the Middle Ages chess remained a recreation of the nobility and well-to-do, and good players, like other artists in those times, often found rich patrons to support them.

The big advances in education in the nineteenth century resulted in the game being much more widely played, and easier travel made possible contests between the best players of different countries. The first World Championship match was held in London in 1866 and since then there has been a rapid rise in the level of play.

Naturally, there are and have been many great players. Mostly these have been European, but our so-called 'European chess' is now played all over the world. National teams from 140 nations compete in the chess 'olympics' which are held regularly.

One could make a long list of famous and clever people of the past who have been keen chessplayers but few, if any, were expert by our present standards; even Napoleon found the chessmen much more difficult to control than his armies. Skill at the game does not seem to go with any special talents, a fact from which most of us can draw encouragement.

The most important and exciting change in the history of chess has, however, taken place in our time: the game has been captured by the young. At any important gathering, including the principal international tournaments, it is youth that now holds the stage and will probably still do so thirteen hundred years hence. The UK Chess Challenge, in which over 65,000 school-children take part, is the largest chess tournament in the world.

This book is for the young, and even for the very young with some guidance from parent or teacher, but it is also for the adult who prefers to tread surely and does not wish to have his intellect stretched in a game. In the arrangement of the contents I have allowed myself to be guided by past pupils, for the beginner knows best the pace he can make and the method and sequence of instruction that suits him.

My aim throughout has been to keep the explanations as simple as possible, so at times I have chosen to state general truths rather than to go into detailed, if more precise descriptions. I doubt if readers will find this book at all difficult to follow, but would like to hear from any who do.

PART ONE

The Rules of Play

1
The Game

Chess is a game of skill between two players. It is played on a chessboard of 64 squares (8 × 8) coloured alternately light and dark. Each player has at his command a small army of chessmen; one is light-coloured, the other dark. The squares of the chessboard, and the chessmen, are usually white and black and are so called whatever their colour. Also, the player of the white men is called White and the player of the black men, Black.

2

At the start of a game, the chessmen are placed on the board in what is called the INITIAL POSITION. Each player moves in turn, White starting. A move is the transfer of a man from the square on which it stands to another square to which it is permitted to move. If an enemy man is standing on the square to which the move is made, then this man is captured: it is removed from the board and takes no further part in the game. Thus in a chess game the number of men on the board is reduced from time to time but never increased. No two men may occupy the same square, nor may a player capture one of his own men.

3
The Chessmen

The men on each side at the start of a game number sixteen: One KING, one QUEEN, two ROOKS (sometimes wrongly called Castles), two BISHOPS, two KNIGHTS and eight PAWNS. They look like this in most chess sets:

| King | Queen | Rook | Bishop | Knight | Pawn |

They look like this in most diagrams:

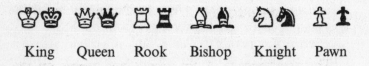

| King | Queen | Rook | Bishop | Knight | Pawn |

Each man moves in a different way, but all men of the same type move in the same way. A (chess) man can mean either a PAWN or a PIECE. Notice that a pawn is not called a piece, and therefore the forces on each side at the start of a game number EIGHT PAWNS and EIGHT PIECES.

4   *Object of the Game*

The object of the game is to capture the opponent's
king, and the first player to do so is the winner. There
are, however, a number of other ways in which a game
can end, either as a win for one side or as a draw.

5   *Initial Position*

Here is the chessboard and the initial position. Each
player ('White' and 'Black' in the diagrams) sits behind
his own army. Observe that the board is placed so that
there is a dark square in the left-hand corner in front of
each player.

(Black)   (Black)

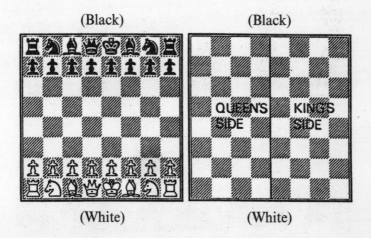

(White)   (White)

The arrangement of the pawns and pieces on the
board is easy to see. Note that the queen is placed on the
square of her own colour (white queen on light square,
black queen on dark square) and the king on the
opposite colour (white king on dark square, black king
on light square). All you need remember is QUEEN ON
SQUARE OF OWN COLOUR since the king must occupy the

remaining square. In most chess diagrams, WHITE is shown as playing UP the board and BLACK down the board.

6

A few chess terms are now necessary. If an imaginary line is drawn down the middle of the board from top to bottom, both queens are seen to be on one side and both kings on the other. The half of the board in which the queens stand in the initial position is called the QUEEN'S SIDE and the half in which the kings stand, the KING'S SIDE. White's king's side is therefore on his right, Black's king's side on his left. These descriptions are never changed, even when the kings and queens move around the board. See page 11.

7   *Files and Ranks*

The lines of squares that run up and down the board are called, appropriately enough for a war game, the FILES; and those that run across the board, the RANKS.

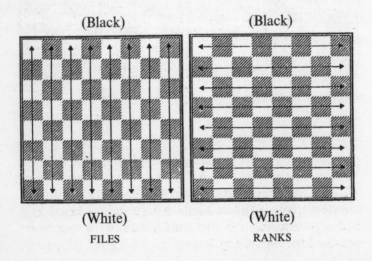

(Black)   (Black)

(White)   (White)

FILES   RANKS

One also talks of DIAGONALS. There are 26 on the board, varying in length from two to eight squares as shown in the diagram below. Each diagonal is made up of squares of one colour only, whereas files and ranks have squares of alternating colours.

The CENTRE is a term used to refer to the four central squares and, more loosely, the twelve squares around them. The importance of the centre in chess will become clear later.

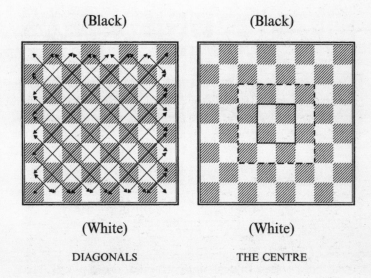

(Black)   (Black)

(White)   (White)

DIAGONALS   THE CENTRE

9

We now consider the separate chessmen. The moves of the king, queen, rook and bishop are easy to understand and it is only those of the knight and pawn that may prove a little difficult at first.

The Rook and Bishop

The ROOK moves in straight lines, vertical and horizontal (that is, along the ranks and files) and the BISHOP along the diagonals in any direction. A rook or bishop may be moved to any vacant square along any of the lines on which it stands provided that, in moving to the chosen square, there are no men of either colour in its path. If a rook or bishop may legally move to a square which is occupied by an enemy man, then that man can be captured and is at once removed from the board.

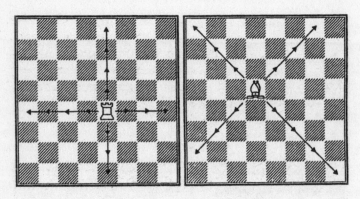

Rook's Move   Bishop's Move

It will be seen that, if unobstructed, these pieces have great freedom of action, being able to cross the board in a single move. Each move, however, may only be made in one direction. On an empty board, a rook, wherever placed, could move immediately to any one of 14 squares, and could reach any other square on the board in two moves and in each case would have two ways of doing this.

You should prove this to yourself before going further.

The bishop, because it moves on diagonals, keeps to the squares of one colour throughout the game. The bishop controls most squares (13) if posted in the centre and fewest squares (7) if on the edge of the board. Again, prove this statement to yourself.

Because the bishop can move on squares of one colour only, enemy men occupying squares on the opposite colour are safe from attack by it. Look again at the initial position and you will see that at the start of a game each player has one bishop on a white square and one on a black.

11 *Capturing*

Capturing in chess is optional. To capture an opponent's man for nothing is usually good for it means that his army is thereby reduced in strength compared with yours. This in turn will reduce his resistance thus making your task that much easier.

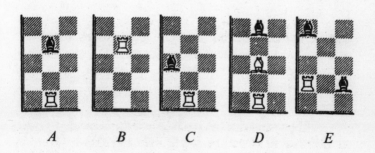

A   B   C   D   E

In many diagrams in this book only a part of the chessboard is shown to save space. The edges of the board are always shown where necessary.

In *A*, the white rook is attacking the black bishop. If it is White's turn to play, he can capture it. *B* shows the position on completion of the capture. The black bishop has been removed from the board. If it was Black's turn to move in *A*, he could escape by removing his bishop from the line of attack as, for example, in *C*. The bishop cannot attack the rook for it is on a white square. In *D*, the rook is not attacking the black bishop because there is a white bishop in the way. Were this piece to move, the rook would then be attacking the black bishop. In *E*, White, to play, could capture either bishop. If neither bishop moved (suppose Black plays somewhere else on the board), the rook could capture both of them in three moves and would have four different ways of doing this. You may care to work these out.

Do not try to memorize these or other diagrams for they are only examples. Try instead to learn the ideas. The positions in the diagrams you may never see again but the ideas they illustrate will recur many times in your games.

12

A man that is 'attacking' a square occupied by a friendly man is said to be defending or guarding it, since if his companion is captured, he will be able to retake the capturing man.

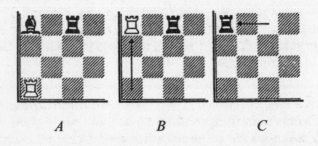

A	*B*	*C*

In *A*, the white rook is attacking the bishop which is defended by a rook. If White, on his turn to play, takes the bishop (*B*), Black can then recapture the rook (*C*). White has lost a rook and Black has lost a bishop.

13

Here are some mini-positions that will help you understand the rooks better and generally how chessmen move, attack and defend each other.

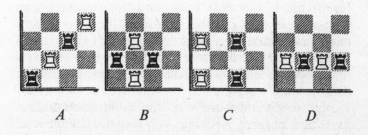

A   B   C   D

In *A*, no rook attacks or defends any other. In *B*, no rook is attacked but rooks of the same colour defend each other. In *C*, each rook defends his twin and attacks an enemy rook. Neither side can win a piece in this situation whoever is to move and regardless of what move is made (to 'win a piece' means to capture it for nothing). This may seem incredible, but try it! In *D*, each side has the option of 3 captures and whoever moves first wins a rook by making any capture. This would be true however the four rooks were arranged on the same rank or file. Again, convince yourself that this statement is correct.

14   *Exchanging*

Where a man is captured and a similar man is given up for it (a rook for a rook; a bishop for a bishop) there has been no loss to either side. This is called an EXCHANGE, and we talk of 'exchanging rooks' for example.

15

If you have anyone to play with (you can even play against yourself), you can now try your skill. Place the board with a dark square in the left-hand corner (remember!) and put the four rooks and four bishops on it so that no piece attacks an opposing piece (this is a good exercise in itself). White moves first and the winner is the player who is a piece ahead *when it is his turn to play*. This is a simple game and, like noughts and crosses, it is only possible to win if the other player makes an elementary mistake. It is a rule of chess that if you touch a man when it is your turn to play then you must move it, and if you touch one of your opponent's men, you must capture it if you can. It is good practice to play 'touch and move' at all times. Once you make a move and let go of your man, you may not change your move.

If you keep hold of the man you may play it to some other square if you wish but you must move it ('touch and move'). It is best to think out your move and then play firmly without hesitation.

16

Chess pieces in their movements form patterns. These patterns show the relationship between the different men and the limits that the chessboard places on them.

Below, and elsewhere in this Part, short problems are given in which you will be able to discover these patterns for yourself and so come to appreciate the strengths and weaknesses of the various men. This will help you to see deeper into the game and play better.

There are several possible solutions to each problem, none of them difficult. Examples are illustrated at the end of the Part.

Construct I   Place the white rooks and bishops (one of these on each colour) so that no piece guards any other.

Construct II   Arrange the same four men so that each piece defends, and is defended by, one other piece.

17 *The Queen and King*

The QUEEN'S move is a combination of those of rook and bishop. The queen can therefore move in any direction in a straight line. She is the most powerful piece on the board.

The KING moves like the queen but only one square at a time. A king thus commands eight squares if not on the edge of the board, five squares on the edge and three squares if he is standing in a corner.

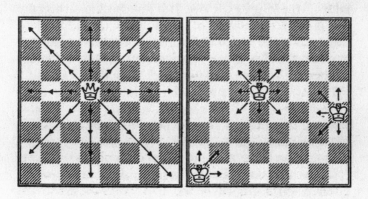

Queen's Move   King's Move

18 *Check and Checkmate*

We have said that the object of the game is to capture the opponent's king. A king which is attacked and therefore threatened with capture on the next move is said to be in CHECK. When you attack your opponent's king say 'Check'; it is a good practice though not compulsory.

If the king is unable to escape from a check it is CHECKMATE and the game is over.

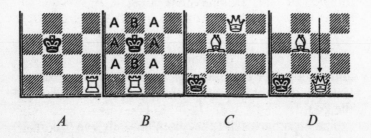

A   B   C   D

In *A*, the white rook moves and puts the black king in check (*B*). It is check because the rook is threatening to take off the king next move. It is not checkmate because the king has a choice of six squares (marked A) to which to move to escape capture. The king may not move to the two squares marked (B) because on either of these he would still be in check from the rook.

It is a rule that the side whose king is in check must immediately get out of check. There are three possible ways of doing this, all or any of which may be playable in a given position:

(1) The king may move to a square which is not attacked by an enemy man;
(2) The man giving check may be captured;
(3) A defender may be placed between the attacker and the king.

If none is possible, then the king is checkmate and the game is over.

In *C* the white queen moves to give check (*D*). Black cannot escape this check as the three squares to which the king could normally move are attacked either by the queen or the bishop. The position is checkmate. The black king is lost and the game is over.

While checkmate is always the best move you can make in a game, a move that gives check is not necessarily good or bad. Many beginners make the mistake of giving check whenever they can, possibly because they enjoy announcing it.

19

You will now be aware that the king is never actually captured in chess: the game is over when one side cannot avoid loss of his king on the next move. In other respects, the king may move and capture like any other piece. He cannot, of course, capture a defended man because by so doing he would be moving into check. *The two kings cannot stand next to each other because they would both then be in check.* This is an important consideration towards the end of the game as we shall see.

20

The following mini-positions will help you further to understand 'check' and 'checkmate'.

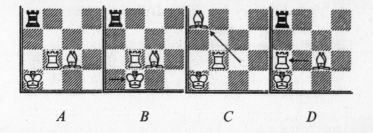

| A | B | C | D |

In *A*, the white king is in check from the black rook. White must now get out of check at once. He may move the king (*B*), capture the attacking piece with his bishop (*C*) or interpose a rook (*D*), as he pleases. Here is another situation:

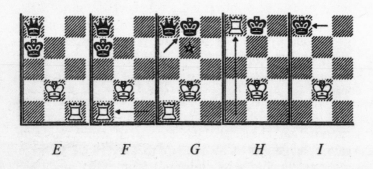

E   F   G   H   I

White moves in *E* and checks the black king (*F*). The king moves out of check (*G*) since the attacker could not be captured and no man could be interposed anyway. Note that the king had an alternative square (marked *) to which he could have moved to escape the check. In *H*, the rook has captured the queen, again giving check to the black king. In *I*, the king recaptures the rook; a legal move since the piece was not defended. The king has not been checkmated but Black has lost a queen for a rook. Lastly, a sequence of moves ending in checkmate:

J   K   L

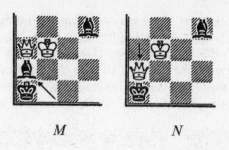

M   N

In *J*, the white queen has just given check. The only
way Black can escape the check is to interpose the
bishop (*K*): he cannot move his king forward as it would
then stand next to the white king, which is illegal. In *L*,
the queen, moving like a bishop, has again checked the
black king. *M* shows the position after Black's only
move: again interposing the bishop and at the same time
giving check to the white king. *N* shows the end of the
game. The queen, moving like a rook, has captured the
black bishop simultaneously releasing the white king
from check and checkmating the black king. The king
cannot take the queen as the queen is defended by the
white king. It may help you to play this sequence
through again. Can you see the defensive role of the
bishop that does not move? White has forced a MATE
(checkmate is usually simply called 'mate') in three
moves.

21

Here are a few more problems to help you become
familiar with the pieces we have studied. Again, all are
on the quarter-board.

Construct III   Place four white queens so that none
                  is defended (you can use pawns to
                  represent queens).

Construct IV	Construct checkmate positions using both kings and, in turn, the following white men: (1) Queen and rook; (2) Queen; (3) Two rooks; (4) Rook and bishop; (5) Rook; (6) Two bishops.
Construct V	Arrange a king, queen, rook and bishop of each colour so that no man of either side is attacked.

22   *The Knight*

We shall return to checkmate later, but let us now look at the KNIGHT. The knight is the most attractive of chess pieces, both in appearance and on account of its move. The knight's move may be described in different ways:

(1) As the letter 'L';
(2) The next square but one of a different colour;
(3) One square horizontally or vertically, then one square diagonally in the same direction;
(4) The opposite corner of a 3 × 2 rectangle.

Knight's Move

In these three positions, the knight's move is to any of the starred squares. The knight moves directly to the chosen square: it does not follow a path like the queen, rook or bishop. This is an important feature of the knight for it means that its movement cannot be blocked by other men. It will be seen from the diagrams that the knight's power is reduced near or at the edge of the board and is further reduced next to or in a corner. The knight always attacks squares of the opposite colour to the square on which it stands. Each move therefore the knight 'changes colour'. The knight captures in a similar way to the other pieces.

The knight's freedom of movement is well shown in *A*. Despite being surrounded by black men, it can escape to any of eight squares, although only on one of these squares will it not be attacked. Can you see which one?

Although free to move, a knight is weak at close quarters for it attacks none of the adjoining squares. In *B*, all the white pieces are attacking the knight. Furthermore, it cannot escape as all six squares to which it may move are controlled by the white queen.

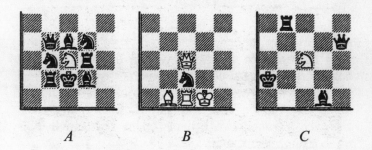

A   *B*   *C*

In *C*, the knight attacks all the black men simultaneously. The king, which is in check, will have to move when the knight will be free to capture one of the black pieces. This example shows the knight at its best.

23

Before you try some more problems, look again at CONSTRUCT III. If you solved this, you will now see that the four queens were separated from each other by knight moves.

Construct VI   Put any four of the five white pieces (king, queen, rook, bishop and knight) on a quarter-board so that no man guards any other. Try each combination of pieces in turn.

Construct VII   Place a white king, bishop and knight so that the knight has no move.

Construct VIII   Set up a checkmate position using a king and a knight of each colour.

Construct IX   Place the eight black pieces on a quarter-board together with the white king so that White is not in check and has a choice of three captures.

Construct X   Arrange the two kings together with a white queen, rook, bishop and knight so that each of the four white pieces can mate in one move.

24
The Pawn

This brings us to the PAWN, a man often scorned by beginners but treasured by the experts.

The pawn moves FORWARD only, ONE square at a time along the file on which it stands. Each pawn may, however, advance TWO squares on its first move. This double jump is optional.

Unlike the pieces, the pawn captures in a different way from which it moves. The pawn attacks the two squares diagonally forward, one on either side, unless the pawn stands on the edge of the board when it attacks only one square. The capture is carried out in

the same manner as with the pieces: the pawn moves on
to the square occupied by the enemy man, which is
removed from the board.

In *A*, the white pawn can move one or two squares as
its position indicates that it has not moved from the
start of the game (as a pawn moves only forward, it is
not possible for it to have moved and then returned to
its original square). The black pawn in *A* can move only
one square forward as it has clearly already moved. In
B, neither pawn can move. A pawn, like all other men,
can only move onto an occupied square to capture –
and pawns do not capture vertically forward. In *C*,
either pawn may move one square forward or capture
the opposing pawn, depending on whose move it is.

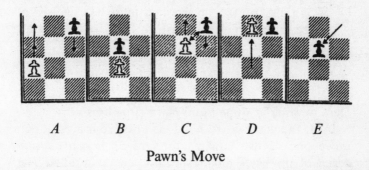

A   B   C   D   E

Pawn's Move

A special situation is illustrated in *D*. The white pawn
has just made the initial double move. *The black pawn
may now capture it as though it had only moved one
square. E* shows the position after the capture, with the
white pawn removed from the board. This special move
is called EN PASSANT (French for 'in passing') and can
only take place between two pawns. The capture must be
made at once (that is, on the next move) or this right is
lost. An 'en passant' capture is optional.

As this move is the one that gives most trouble to beginners, repetition may help:

(1) The 'en passant' move can only take place after the initial two-square move of a pawn;
(2) The capture can be made only by an opposing pawn that could legally have captured the adversary if it had moved one square;
(3) The capture is made by placing the capturing pawn on the square over which his victim has passed, removing the captured pawn from the board. You will see that this move is similar to an orthodox pawn capture: one square diagonally forward. This is the only case in chess where a man making a capture moves to a square other than that occupied by the man being captured;
(4) The right to take 'en passant' must be exercised at once or the privilege is lost.

25

Here we look at some more pawn situations.

In *A*, the white pawn has four possible moves: it can move one or two squares forward or it can capture either of the black men. In *B*, no pawn can move. The middle pawn could only have got where it is by making a capture from its initial square. The white pawns are said to be DOUBLED. It is not uncommon to have three pawns of the same colour on one file.

All four pawns in *C* can only move to capture, and each has one available capture. Black is threatening to take off the white pawn in *D*. White can evade the threat by advancing the free pawn one square, when all four pawns will be without a move (*E*) or by capturing the black pawn. If the white pawn takes the black pawn, the second black pawn could recapture when there would be only two pawns left – one of each colour – neither of which will be able to move. We are back to position *B* in the previous section.

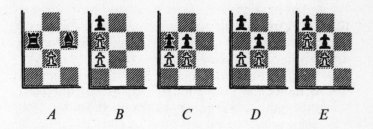

A	*B*	*C*	*D*	*E*

26 Pawn Promotion

You may be wondering what happens to a pawn when it arrives at the end of the board (if you have read *Alice Through the Looking Glass* you will already know!). A pawn on reaching the last rank is promoted to any piece, *other than a king*, at the player's choice. Promotion is compulsory – it cannot remain a pawn. The promotion is made by placing the piece chosen on the promotion square and removing the pawn from the board. If the pawn on promotion simultaneously captures an enemy piece, then of course this piece is also taken off the board.

Since the queen is the most powerful piece, a pawn is almost invariably promoted to queen (the promotion square is often called the QUEENING SQUARE). The move is completed by promotion, and thereafter the promoted piece behaves in the same manner as a queen (or whatever piece is chosen).

The pieces remaining on the board at the time of promotion do not affect the choice of piece. It is not unusual in a game for one side to have two queens on the board; nine are possible but unheard of! (If you don't have a second queen to hand, substitute an inverted rook or a token.)

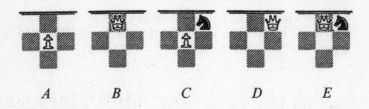

A   B   C   D   E

A–B shows the promotion of a pawn to queen; *A* before the move and *B* on completion of the move. *C–D* is the same sequence but this time the pawn promotes in making a capture. Notice that the pawn could also have been promoted by moving straight forward one square (*E*).

Now you will see why pawns are not to be scorned: each one is a potential queen. A pawn's journey to promotion is a long one and is unlikely to be achieved until most of the pieces are gone from the board. The side that 'queens a pawn' first is often in a position to win quickly.

27

Back now to a few problems on the quarter-board.

Construct XI	Place eight pawns (four of each colour) so that none may move or capture.
Construct XII	Place the same eight pawns so that each side has six different captures.
Construct XIII	Arrange the two kings and one white pawn so that white can promote and give checkmate in one move.
Construct XIV	Set up a checkmate position, without promotion, using only king and one pawn of each colour.

Construct XV	Construct a position in which a pawn can play to any one of four squares and is at no time attacked.
Construct XVI	Construct a position in which one pawn may make any one of twelve different moves and is at no time itself attacked (if you solved XV you have practically solved this!).

28 *Values of the Men*

You may already have formed an opinion about the worth of some of the chessmen. Here is a table of relative values:

Pawn–1 Knight–3 Bishop–3 Rook–5 Queen–9

No value is given to the king since he cannot be exchanged. His powers are about equal to those of a knight or bishop.

The values given are only approximate (in fact, two bishops are much better than rook and pawn although both count six points) but you should be guided by them when making captures and exchanges. For example, if you give up your queen for rook, bishop and three pawns, you will see that this is to your advantage (nine points against eleven). Later you will see how the values of the men vary even from move to move, according to the position.

29

A few more common terms may be useful here:

The queen and rooks are known as MAJOR PIECES.

The bishops and knights are known as MINOR PIECES.

To gain a rook for the loss of a knight or bishop is to WIN THE EXCHANGE.

30 *Castling*

There is a special move in chess that both players may make once in every game. This special move is called

CASTLING. Two men – the king and one rook – which must be on their original squares, move together, the single exception to the rule that only one man may move at a time.

Castling consists of moving the king two squares towards the rook and then bringing the rook to the square next to the king on the inside. It is a rule that the king shall be moved first when castling.

When this double move takes place on the king's side, it is called king's side castling, and on the queen's side, queen's side castling.

KING'S SIDE CASTLING   QUEEN'S SIDE CASTLING

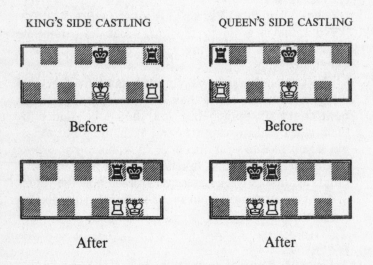

Before   Before

After   After

A player may castle at any time provided that certain conditions are met:

(1) The king and the chosen rook have not been moved.
(2) There is no man of either colour between the king and the rook.

(3) The king is not in check at the time, nor will he in castling pass through check, nor will he be in check when castling is completed.

A, B, C and *D* illustrate four cases where castling is not possible. *A* – the rook has moved; *B* – the king is in check; *C* – the king would pass through check; *D* – the king would be in check on completion of castling.

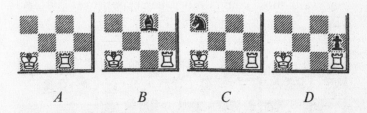

| A | B | C | D |

Castling achieves two things:

(1) It removes the king from the middle of the board where it is in most danger.
(2) It brings a rook from the corner into the centre where the piece is more active.

Castling is optional, and there is no such move as 'uncastling'. The right to castle should not be given up easily as it is a very useful move. Castling is used by both players in most games.

It is a common belief that once a king has been checked it may not castle. This is not so, as the above rules should make clear.

31 *Stalemate and Zugzwang*

To close our review of the main rules of the game, mention must be made of a situation which is sometimes reached where a side whose turn it is to play has no legal move. This situation is known as STALEMATE and is only likely to occur when there are few men left on the board. Stalemate is a draw, and the game is over.

A player cannot choose not to move just because it would lead to certain loss. If there is a legal move on the board it must be made. This situation, which does not end the game, is known as ZUGZWANG (German: 'forced move'). Stalemate is quite common among beginners (particularly where one side has only a king left), zugzwang more common between experienced players.

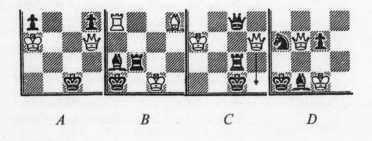

A   *B*   *C*   *D*

A typical stalemate position is shown at *A*. Black, to move, is unable to do so. In *B*, Black, to move, is again stalemated as neither the rook nor the bishop can move without exposing the king to check, whilst the king may not move next to the white king. With White to play, however, the game is checkmate as White can take the rook off with the bishop which is then defended by the king. The black king is in check and has no escape. White is a rook behind in *C* and his king is in peril – normally a hopeless position. However, he can here save the game by an ingenious sacrifice, as shown. The black king must take the queen as it is the only legal move – and White is then stalemated! *D* is an amusing example of zugzwang. Black, who is not threatened with an immediate checkmate, is forced to move. Whichever man he moves he is checkmated next play. The mates are worth working out as they demonstrate the great power of the queen.

32

Finally, a few more quarter-board exercises.

Construct XVII   Place a black king, bishop & pawn and a white king & bishop so that Black is stalemated.

Construct XVIII   Set up a stalemate position using a white king & pawn and the two black rooks and putting no man on the edge of the board.

Construct XIX   Arrange any men so that White can play pawn takes pawn 'en passant', at the same time giving checkmate.

Construct XX   Arrange any men so that White can play Castles, at the same time giving checkmate.

33   *Examples of Construction Problems*

Overleaf are example answers to construction problems given in this Part. Other solutions to those shown are possible in most cases. Remember that these problems were designed to exercise your understanding of the various pieces and their behaviour – they do NOT represent positions you are ever likely to see in games. The Roman numeral below each diagram corresponds to the problem number in the text. If you found these difficult, it will be helpful to compare each problem with the given solution.

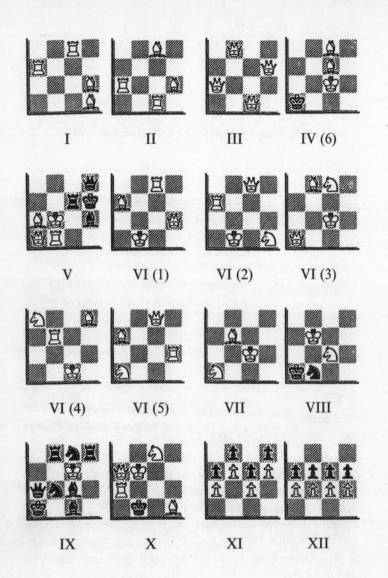

I II III IV (6)

V VI (1) VI (2) VI (3)

VI (4) VI (5) VII VIII

IX X XI XII

36

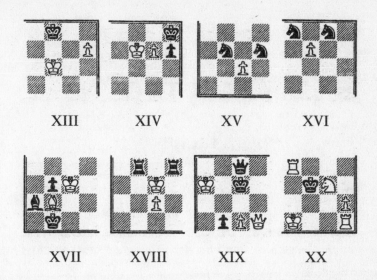

XIII   XIV   XV   XVI

XVII   XVIII   XIX   XX

PART TWO

Tactics

34

All the important rules of the game have now been explained and we are ready to examine tactics – the battles large and small between the two armies in close contact with each other.

The main aims of play we have already discussed. Foremost, to checkmate the opponent's king for this is the object of the game. Secondly, to try to *win material* – to capture men for nothing or to capture men of greater value than you lose. The purpose in winning material is to make it easier to force mate. The more material you win, clearly the easier it will be to do this.

35 *Combinations*

We have seen briefly how the different men work together and in opposition. It is now time to look at ways of winning material and of forcing checkmate. Certain simple manoeuvres, or *combinations* as they are called in chess, occur frequently. In fact, even the most complex play can be reduced to one or other of several basic combinations. These combinations are quite easy to understand in their bare outlines but the situations in which they arise are usually confused by the presence of other men that have no part in the particular manoeuvre. Combinations then, although familiar, have to be looked for, like objects hidden in a puzzle picture. However, it is not enough to wait idly for combinations to turn up; you will try to direct your play to make favourable combinations possible. The basic positions given in the rest of this Part will be repeated again and again in your games although not necessarily in the exact forms you see them here. You will soon know them all well.

36 *Threatened Men*

We have already met attack and defence in its simplest form in section 11.

Let us look at it again in a little more depth.

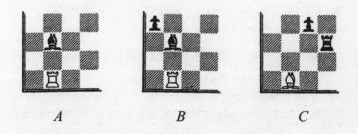

A   *B*   *C*

The situation in *A* is one of the most common in chess and may occur several times during the course of a game. One man attacks another man with the intention of capturing it next move. In *A* the rook has just moved to attack the bishop. We call this a THREAT as it threatens to win the bishop for nothing. The bishop is said to be EN PRISE (French: in a position to be taken).

In *B* there is no threat as the bishop is defended by a pawn (which, you will recall, captures diagonally forward). To capture the bishop would now cost White his rook, which would be a bad move as a rook is worth more than a bishop.

In *C*, the bishop has just moved to attack the rook. This is a threat because although the rook is defended, it is worth more than the bishop and White on his next play will capture it, given the opportunity.

37

There are a number of ways to meet a simple threat:

(*a*) The man making the threat may be captured;
(*b*) The man under attack may move away;
(*c*) A friendly man may be placed between the attacker
       and the man attacked.

These ways of answering a threat are the same as those
open to a player whose king is in check. This is not
surprising as a check is no more than a simple threat to
the king. However, there is no obligation here to rescue
the attacked man, so that two further possibilities are
open to the defender:

(*d*) The attacked man may be defended if it is of equal
       or lesser value than the attacker;
(*e*) The threat may be ignored if it appears that there is
       a better move elsewhere on the board. A man given
       up in this way is said to be *sacrificed*. Sacrifices are
       the sugar and spice of chess, as you will discover.

38

A man that is defended once may be attacked twice –
that is, by two enemy men. This means that the defender
will lose both his men in exchange for only one attacker.
If the attacker is worth less than these two men together,
then a threat exists.

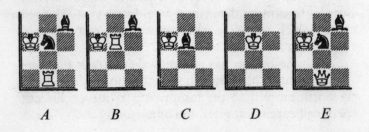

A　　　B　　　C　　　D　　　E

A–D should make this clear. In *A*, White has two men attacking the knight which is defended once. Since bishop and knight are together worth six points and a rook only five, White is threatening to capture the knight.

If Black does nothing about this, the sequence of moves *B–D* follows. In *E*, White again has two men attacking the knight, but since the queen is worth nine points against the six of bishop and knight together, Black is not threatened here.

39

Sometimes both sides build up their forces around one man, often a pawn. Although a number of men may be involved, the same principle applies: if, in a series of exchanges, the defender will lose more than the attacker, a threat exists.

In *A*, White has four men attacking the advanced pawn whilst Black has only three men defending it (notice that the second black rook is only indirectly defending the pawn: he cannot take part in the battle until his companion has engaged the enemy – this second rook acts rather like a reserve waiting in the rear).

A   B

Further, the black men are together valued at 14 points against 11 points for the white men (excluding the king, which cannot of course be captured). White is therefore threatening to capture the pawn. The capture would be made by either knight or bishop. If it were made by the white rook, the black knight would recapture and Black would then break off the engagement. Remember that capturing is not compulsory and neither side need make an unfavourable capture. Now look at *B*. Again White has four men attacking the pawn and only three black men defending it, but here the value of the attacking force is much greater than that of the defending force. If a white piece now takes the pawn, White will lose material so there is no threat to the pawn in the position given.

40

A move may threaten not just one man, but two or sometimes more men. This is a double or multiple threat and is much more dangerous than a simple threat because it is harder to defend.

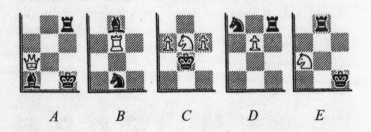

| A | B | C | D | E |

These are examples of double and multiple threats. In *A*, the queen attacks both bishop and rook simultaneously, one of which will be captured next move. In *B*, the rook attacks both bishop and knight. Only one can escape. In *C*, the king has got behind the pawns and is attacking three men at once. Only one man can move to safety and Black will then have the choice of capturing either of the remaining two. In *D*, a pawn attacks both a rook and a knight.

Again, a piece is lost, only this time the attacker will die also as the rook can be moved away so as to maintain the guard on the knight. In *E*, the knight attacks both the king and the rook. The king is in check, so must move when the knight will capture the rook for nothing. These last two examples are known as FORKS since the attack resembles the prongs of a fork. A multiple fork was shown in **22***C*.

41

Possible defences against multiple threats may suggest themselves. The plan open to Black in **40***D* above, although of little help there, would have been good in **40***A* if the black king had not been present. This should be clear in *A–B* below: one of the attacked pieces moves away to defend the other one. Another idea would be to move one of the men attacked to make a threat elsewhere. *C–D* is an example. The knight has forked the two rooks but one of these is able to escape with a check, forcing the black king to move, when the second rook will be moved to safety – a good example of a useful check.

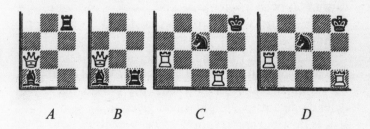

| *A* | *B* | *C* | *D* |

42   *The Pin*
Yet another idea might be to prevent the attacking man from moving. This is a common tactic known as a PIN.

A pin describes a situation where a man may not move, or may not move freely, because of the action of an enemy piece.

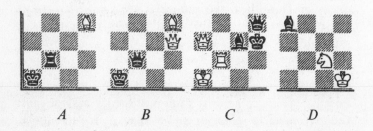

A   B   C   D

In *A*, the rook may not move at all because the king would then be in check from the bishop with White to move, which is forbidden. The rook is said to be pinned – an appropriate description. The queen in *B* can move, but only on the line of the bishop as otherwise the black king would be in check. The queen is said to be pinned even though she has some movement. In *A* and *B*, Black can free himself from the pin by moving his king. However, this will not save him for White will then capture at once in each case and Black is certain to lose material – a rook for a bishop in *A* and a queen for a bishop in *B*.

We have already had an example of pins: look back to **31***B* and you will see that the black rook and bishop are both pinned. We can now add the pin to the list of defences against a simple threat given in **37**.

It is possible for a pinning piece to be itself pinned, as the black bishop in *C*. White could now free the rook by moving his king and the rook could not be captured as the bishop is pinned. If Black in turn frees himself from the pin by moving his king, White will have time to move his rook to safety.

44

D shows the most common type of pin – bishop against knight. There is no threat in this case as the knight, which is worth about the same as the bishop, is guarded. However, a pin like this cannot be said to be harmless because whereas the attacker is active, the pinned piece is, for the time being, useless – it is a 'non-piece'!

43

So far we have examined pins where it is illegal for the pinned piece to move or to move off a line. But a man that may legally move freely is also said to be pinned if it cannot be moved without loss of some kind.

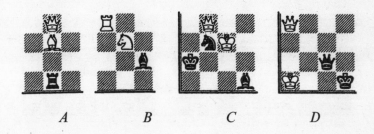

A   *B*   *C*   *D*

If in *A* the bishop moves, the queen is lost. Note that in the position the rook is not threatening the bishop as that piece is guarded by the queen. The bishop is said to be pinned. Here the queen could free the pin by moving to any of the four next-door squares, keeping guard on the bishop.

The knight is pinned in *B* because, if it moves, the bishop will take the rook. Further, the bishop threatens the knight. Here White can free himself by moving the rook to one of the two squares where it guards the knight.

In *C* also the knight is pinned as, if it moves, the white queen will give checkmate at once. *D* illustrates a position that sometimes causes confusion. The white king cannot move even though the black queen is pinned. A pinned piece may still give check (and it is even possible for it to give checkmate if the pinning piece is itself pinned!).

44

A multiple threat may take the form of a simultaneous attack by two (rarely more) pieces. In *A*, White is attacking neither of the black pieces; but after moving (*B*) both black pieces are attacked and one is lost. The power of the DISCOVERED ATTACK, as this tactic is called, can be considerable.

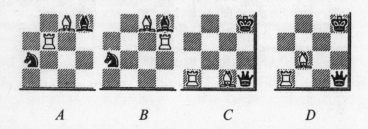

A   B   C   D

C illustrates a more dangerous form of the discovered attack: the piece that moves gives check (*D*). As Black must move his king, the queen is lost.

Opposite are two further types of discovered attack. Look at *E*. Here the king would be in check from the rook if the rook were not masked by the bishop. Since any move of the bishop will require that the rook check be answered, the bishop can be considered to have a 'free' move. Black loses the knight to a bishop attack. This is called a DISCOVERED CHECK.

E F G

F shows an attack directed wholly against the king. Again, a masking piece moves to discover check (*G*), but this time the piece that moves also attacks the king. This is a DOUBLE CHECK. Although both the attacking pieces here are under attack themselves, neither can be captured as this would still leave the king in check from the remaining piece. Again, Black could interpose a piece between the king and either of the attackers but could not cover both attacks in the one move. In reply to a double check therefore *the King must move*. In the example the king has no move and so the position is checkmate.

45

Overleaf at *A* is this same position but without the black knight. Now White would gain nothing by the double check as the black king can move to safety (*B*). Correct for White would be *C* when the black rook would have to play as shown to escape capture. Black has been forced to pin his own rook and White could now 'win the exchange' (**29**) by taking off the rook with the bishop.

But he can do better: the rook is pinned, and White has only to attack with his rook (as for example in *D*) to gain it for nothing next move. This example well illustrates the weaknesses of a pinned piece.

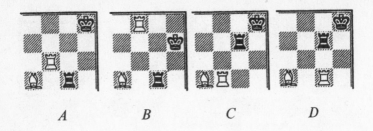

A B C D

46 *The Skewer*

Another common tactical manoeuvre is the SKEWER. Two men, one of which may be the king, are attacked on a line.

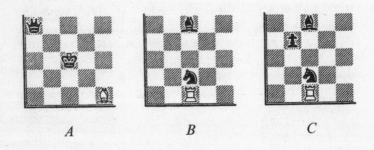

A B C

If the man immediately threatened moves, the second man is lost. *A* and *B* are examples. Compare *B* with **40***B*. In *C*, Black has a sufficient defence in moving up the pawn one square to guard the knight.

47

A pinned man is vulnerable to attack as we saw in **45***D*. Look at *A*, which is similar to **46***C* but with an added white pawn. Black has defended himself against the skewer by advancing the pawn to defend the knight. However, the knight is now pinned and the attack by the white pawn (*B*) wins a piece. Notice, however, that Black can choose which piece to move to safety.

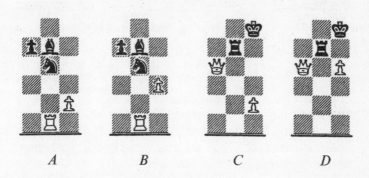

A   B   C   D

C–D is another example of the dangers that threaten pinned men. Here the rook may not legally move so that the pawn advance wins the piece for nothing.

48 *Overworked Men*

Our next diagrams demonstrate a common weakness: overworked men. The pawn in *A* is guarding both the rook and the bishop. White can take advantage of this in the sequence *B–D*, winning the bishop. *E* shows a variation of this: the black queen is defending against a mate and is also guarding the rook. If the rook is captured (*F*), Black cannot retake or he is mated (*G*).

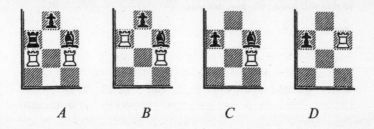

A   B   C   D

E F G

49 *Piece Traps*

A pinned man is without defence and is easily lost but a free man may also be trapped. Traps of this kind have one common feature: the man attacked has no square to which to escape. Different traps catch different men. Below are some of the commonest.

The queen is the hardest piece to trap because escape must be stopped in all directions. A queen that enters the enemy army alone may get into trouble: in *A*, the black queen has unwisely taken a pawn at the same time attacking the rook. Now White shuts the trap with a knight, which also defends the rook (*B*). Next move he will attack the queen with his other knight, when the queen will have no escape. In *C*, if the queen takes the unguarded pawn she is lost for a rook after Black's reply (*D*).

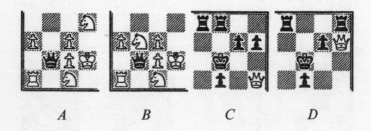

A B C D

These two examples show the most frequent way in which queens are trapped: by the unwise capture of a flank pawn. The queen is rarely trapped in the middle of the board.

50

A rook too is hard to snare. The file on which the rook stands may sometimes be closed by a minor piece (*A–B*). Here a rook falls for bishop and pawn. A rook that can only move along a rank can sometimes be caught with surprising ease. In *C*, the rook has no safe square from the pawn attack.

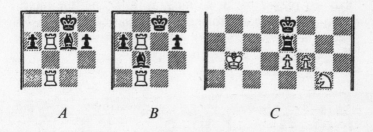

A *B* *C*

51

Bishops are often trapped. Probably the commonest of all piece traps is illustrated in *A–B*. The advance of the white pawns hems in the piece. The trap is seen in many forms but almost always depends on the bishop's retreat being blocked by its own men.

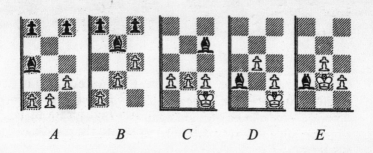

A *B* *C* *D* *E*

A venturesome bishop may fare no better. If the pawn is taken in *C*, White can close the line of retreat (*D*) and next move play the king (*E*) to win the bishop for two pawns.

52

A knight can be caught on the edge of the board in a situation that is common early in the game. In *A*, White has just played the pawn forward, attacking the piece. To move the knight to the side of the board now (*B*) would be a bad mistake, as after another pawn move (*C*) the piece has no square for escape.

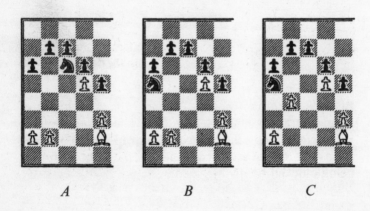

A   *B*   *C*

53

A pawn may also be trapped if it advances too far. Without support from a friendly pawn, it will be lost if a superior force can be brought against it (**39***A*). Consider all pawn advances very carefully: remember, pawns cannot be moved back if danger threatens!

54

You will meet these traps often in your play. If you know them well they will earn you – or save you – many games. A final and important point. If you have the misfortune to have a piece trapped, do not just leave it to be taken off for nothing; capture the best enemy man you can, even if it's only a pawn. For example, in *A* take off the bishop with the rook and in *B* capture the pawn with the knight. If no capture is possible, you may be able to play your man so that your opponent must take it in a way less favourable to him. See *C*; the knight is trapped. Play as in *D* and Black must capture (*E*) or allow the piece to escape. Black's pawns are doubled and weak, as we shall see.

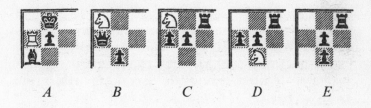

| *A* | *B* | *C* | *D* | *E* |

55   *The Sacrifice*

Sacrifices, we said earlier, add greatly to the pleasure of the game. One can get a lot of satisfaction out of allowing a piece to be captured in order later to force an advantage. One merit of a sacrifice is that it often comes as a surprise to the second player, and the unexpected is always a little disturbing. If your opponent puts (say) a knight 'en prise', you may suspect a trap. What is coming next? In this situation a timid player is frightened into defence, yet the move may be simply a mistake. Even intentional sacrifices are often unsound (that is, they fail against the best defence). Never be afraid to accept a sacrifice if you can see no good reason for it.

A sacrifice is not a means in itself but a means to an end. Here are two examples. In *A*, White has just played the rook on to an undefended square. Since this move is a check and also a double attack such as we saw in **40**, it is forcing, Black's only sensible reply being to capture the rook, when the knight moves (*B*) forking king and queen.

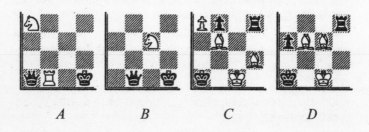

A   *B*   *C*   *D*

See now that the king must move next to the queen in order to recapture the knight after the queen is taken. Even so, White has gained from the combination. In *C*, White has just made the initial two-square move with his pawn. If Black accepts the sacrifice by taking the pawn 'en passant' (**24**), then he is mated (*D*).

56   *Examples of Checkmate*

It is now time to consider some typical checkmate positions and a little of the play that may lead up to them. In order to checkmate, we must do two things at the same time:

(*a*) Put the king in check so that the attacking man cannot be taken and no defending man can be placed between them;

(*b*) Ensure that all the squares around the king are attacked, or are occupied by defenders.

Put like that, it sounds quite difficult, for if the king is away from the edge of the board there are no less than eight squares to cover in addition to the square on which he stands. However, if the king is at the edge of the board there are only five possible escape squares (or *flight squares* as they are sometimes called) and in the corner this number is reduced to three. It is therefore easier still if he is in the corner. It is usually much simpler to drive a king to the side by a series of checks rather than attempt a checkmate in the middle of the board. As it happens, though, the kings tend to spend most of their time at the edge of the board anyway!

57

Broadly speaking, the play leading to checkmate may be of two kinds:

(a) Direct, forceful play, where every move is urgent as the defender will, if given the chance, quickly counter-attack. This type of situation usually occurs in games where forces are about even and one side has succeeded in working up an attack on the king, perhaps at the cost of a sacrifice.

(b) Steady, less anxious play in which the attacker has a much stronger force and the issue is not whether he will be able to force checkmate, but when. A few small inaccuracies in the attack under these circumstances are unimportant as they are only likely to delay the checkmate, not to forfeit it.

58

First let us look at some common mating positions. You should quickly learn to recognize them on sight. Better still, you should try to see them coming so that you can either force them or defend against them.

Notice how the king and queen work together against a bare king (A). Several similar mating positions are possible with these three pieces. Can you find some? B

A   B   C   D

shows the mating position with a rook against a bare king. Observe how the white king guards all the squares to which his rival might move to escape check. These two examples well illustrate the rule that kings may not stand next to each other. In *C* a second rook is doing the same job as the king in *B*. *D* is less common but not unusual. In the last three examples, a queen could of course do the same job as a rook.

59

All the above positions would be most likely to arise under the conditions described in **57(*b*)**. The next are examples of mating positions more likely to arise from forceful play when there are still many men on the board **57(*a*)**. You will see that in each case the king is in the castled position.

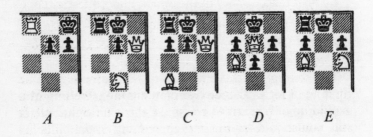

A   B   C   D   E

A is perhaps the commonest of all mating positions. The king is doomed because his natural flight squares are occupied by his own unmoved pawns. All the other

56

| F | G | H |

examples are also common. *H* is a variation of *G*. Both show a well-known mating idea the elements of which are:

(*a*) The king is on the edge of the board;

(*b*) The king is in check from a rook or a queen;

(*c*) The centre one of the three natural flight squares on the next rank or file is occupied by a defender, usually a pawn;

(*d*) The remaining two squares are controlled by an attacker which may be any man except the rook.

60

A feature of all the above examples excepting one is that mate is delivered by a major piece. Mates by the minor pieces, and even pawns, are not rare but the great majority of all checkmates are delivered by queen or rook. The reason for this is that, as well as giving check, the rook usually commands two of the king's flight squares and the queen any number up to four.

The bishop, on the other hand, only commands one when the king is at the edge of the board, the knight a maximum of one anywhere, and the pawn none at all. It may be useful to summarize these few general hints for forcing checkmate:

(*a*) Force the enemy king to the edge of the board or in a corner. This is done by a series of checks.

57

(*b*) Remember that queen and rook are the easiest pieces with which to mate. If your opponent's king is open to attack, get your queen in close to him.

(*c*) If you can advance your king with safety, use him to prevent the escape of the enemy king.

61

Let us now go back a move or two in some of these positions and force checkmate.

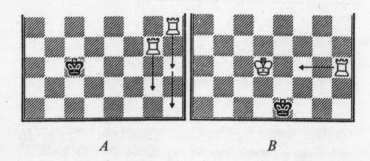

A   *B*

To start with, consider *A* in relation to **58***C*. Here White forces mate by checking with the rooks in turn. The king is forced to the edge of the board where he is mated. If check is given with the wrong rook, the king escapes briefly but can soon be forced back again (try this and see).

A less brutal finish is shown in *B*. White, instead of checking and allowing the king to escape, plays a quiet move to force the black king opposite the white king to reach the mating position in **58***B*. Note that each of the rooks in *A* does the same job in turn that the white king does in *B*: blocking the escape of the black king to the next rank.

62

The next examples give typical play leading to positions similar to those in **59**.

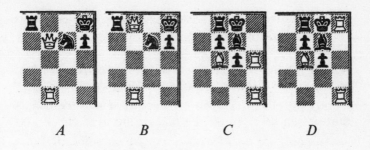

A   B   C   D

A illustrates the idea in **59***A*. White mates by sacrificing the queen (*B*). Now the rook must take the queen, when the white rook recaptures to give checkmate. *C* shows another sacrifice. In this position you can see the outlines of **59***F*. White mates by checking with the rook (*D*). The bishop must capture, when the second rook recaptures.

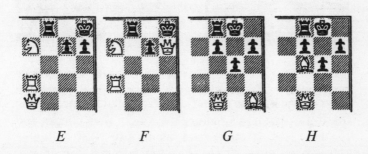

E   F   G   H

Note in *E* the pressure of the white pieces around the king. When one side manages to gather a local superiority of strength like this, a direct attack is quite likely to succeed. White plays as in *F* – a queen sacrifice that breaks open the pawn defences. The king must capture, when the rook moves across to mate – the same type of situation as those in **59***G* and *H*:

The end is not hard to see in *G*. White plays as in *H* and now however Black plays he cannot stop the queen giving mate in at most two moves.

You should be able to work this out without difficulty, but if not, look back to **59**D.

63 *Smothered Mate*

To close our study of mating positions, there is a remarkable finish known as *smothered mate* which is quite often seen. In *A*, the black king is in check and

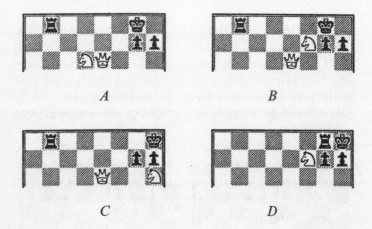

A   B

C   D

must move into the corner or he is mated at once by the queen (look for this mate). The knight then checks and the king has to move back again (*B*). Now a double check once more drives the king into the corner (*C*). White then makes the spectacular move of placing his queen next to the king to give check – a delightful sacrifice. The king cannot take the queen because she is guarded by the knight (which incidentally is itself attacked!) so the rook must do so, when the knight delivers the 'smothered mate' (*D*).

PART THREE

Strategy

64 *Positional Play*

The play we have studied so far has been *tactical* – sharp fighting to checkmate or to win material. But many, if not most moves in a game of chess are strategical – *positional* moves as we call them. Put simply, positional play is aimed at improving one's own position or worsening one's opponent's position, which is much the same thing. A good position is one in which the men are strongly posted for attack or defence, work well together and do not get in one another's way. A bad position, of course, is the opposite.

65

Positional play is not an end in itself: it is preparation for tactical play. An attack is likely to succeed only if it starts from a good position. Positional moves aim at making and enlarging weaknesses in the enemy's position and avoiding them in one's own. A weakness may be *temporary* or *permanent*, but is not strictly a weakness unless the other side can take advantage of it – *exploit* it, we say.

66

Positional play is more difficult than tactical play because its aims are less obvious. However, positional play is like tactical play in that there are a number of common situations the correct handling of which can be easily learned. Often both types of play are mixed together, and although positional play is normally preparation for tactical play, sometimes tactical play is for positional advantage.

67 *Force, Space and Time*

A chess game can be said to be of three elements – the men, the board and the moves, often expressed as *force, space* and *time*. If you have the stronger force (in other words, you are ahead in material), you are more likely to win. Similarly, if you control more of the chessboard than your opponent you will again be better placed to win; and lastly, if you have more moves than your opponent then once again you will have the better chances. But, you may wonder, how can I have more moves than my opponent when each of us plays in turn? Think of the initial position of a pawn. Suppose you move it up one square and next play move it again. These two one-step moves might have been achieved by a single two-square jump. You have 'lost' a move (often called a *tempo*). Another example: you advance a piece and it is attacked by a pawn. If you put your man back where it came from you have lost at least one tempo. Beginners frequently waste time like this.

Force, space and time are constant elements in a game of chess but the value of each may vary with the position and the stage of the game. An advantage in force may be matched by the second player's advantage in space for example, but this could be only a temporary balance. Of the three elements, that of material is probably the most important because it is likely to be the more permanent.

If you are a piece ahead, for example, you are more likely to preserve this advantage – perhaps right to the end of the game – than you are to keep an advantage in, say, time.

68 *Importance of the Centre*

The *centre*, meaning the four central squares and, more loosely, the squares around them (*8*), is most important in chess. The centre is the heart of the chessboard and the main area of battle. From the centre an attack can be turned to left or right much more easily than one can be moved from one side of the board to the other. Control of the centre is usually shared, at least in the early stages of a game. To gain complete control of the centre is often to get a winning advantage.

69

The easiest way to contest the centre is with pawns, and for this reason the usual opening moves for both sides include the advance of one or more of the central pawns. It is not necessary to occupy the centre to contest it however; pieces working from a distance can sometimes do this. To be over-bold in the centre can be as bad as being too timid; however you play though, you must fight for the centre. It is also the best place in which to counter-attack if you are being pressed on one of the wings.

70 *Open and Close Positions*

There are broadly two kinds of position in the period of preparation for the main battle: the *open* position and the *close* position. In the open position, a pawn or two in the centre have probably been exchanged and the pieces have freedom of movement. Open positions encourage tactical play in which the long-stepping pieces are likely to rule. A close position is one in which few if any pawns have been exchanged and the two sides have either kept apart or have become locked together like boxers who can only jab at each other. Knights enjoy close positions because in them they can move more freely than the other pieces and can take long walks to better squares since the time element is of less importance. Many games, however, are neither wholly open nor wholly closed but share features of both types of position. Pictured are two typical positions early in a game.

BLACK

BLACK

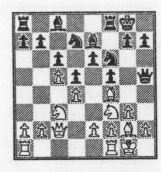

A WHITE

B WHITE

A is an open position in which White has control in the centre and so is well placed for attack. *B* is a close position in which chances are about even.

71 *The Pawn Structure*

We have had to start our study of strategy with a large chunk of theory. Do not worry if you have found this difficult to follow: a few examples will help to make things clearer.

We begin with the pawns because they are very important in positional play. Most weaknesses occur in what we call the *pawn structure* or *pawn skeleton* – the arrangement of the pawns at any particular stage of the game. One reason for this is that no pawn move can be reversed (pawns only go forward, remember) whereas a piece that has been unwisely moved can often be returned to its previous square, even if time is lost. Pawns alone are usually strongest when they stand next to one another on a rank (*A*), and often when they are defending one another in a diagonal line (*B*), particularly when the line points towards the centre of the board. Pawns are a little weaker where a pair is *doubled* on a file (as in *C*) and much weaker when *doubled* and *isolated* (*D*). An isolated pawn is one that has no friendly pawn on a next-door file. A pawn may be *backward*, like the central white pawn in *E*. A backward pawn also cannot be supported by a friendly pawn but for a different reason: its advance is prevented by an enemy man, usually a pawn, that occupies or attacks a square in its path.

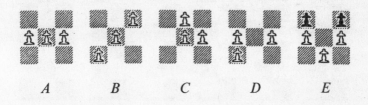

A   B   C   D   E

A pawn weakness need only be temporary: in *D* for example, a capture by the pawn on the dark square would regain the ideal formation shown in *A*.

72

When a pawn is attacked by an enemy piece – a common happening – it may not be possible or convenient to guard it with a friendly man. Under these circumstances the only defence may be to advance the attacked pawn. Look at *A* (overleaf): here a rook attacks doubled and isolated pawns. The weakness of these pawns is obvious: they cannot defend each other and are unable to escape the rook's attack. Two pawns side-by-side are much better placed, as the sequence *B–E* shows. In *B*, the rook attacks one pawn that moves forward a square and is then protected by the other (*C*). The rook attacks the second pawn (*D*), which moves up two squares so as to be defended by its companion (*E*). Now the rook can return to attack the first pawn which can no longer be defended. When the pawn is captured, however, the second pawn will already have reached the fifth rank and, depending on the position elsewhere on the board, may prove dangerous as it is near to promotion.

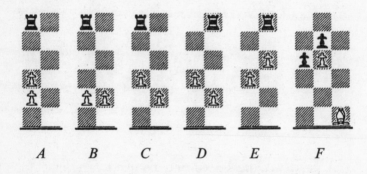

A *B* *C* *D* *E* *F*

In *F*, Black has a *passed* pawn. A passed pawn is one that cannot be stopped by an opposing pawn and may be thought of as the opposite of a backward pawn. A backward pawn is weak, but a passed pawn, particularly if defended as here, is strong because the other side must employ a piece to stop its advance. If, in *F*, the white bishop moves away the passed pawn may race to queen.

Squares controlled by pawns cannot be occupied by pieces of the opposite colour without material loss. As far as possible, therefore, pawns should be used to control squares on which enemy pieces would be well placed – particularly in the centre and around the kings' positions. Pawns in defence are usually strongest if unmoved. It is necessary to protect your king with pawns, and *A–E* show good defences for a castled king, particularly in open or half-open positions (in close positions there may be less danger to the king).

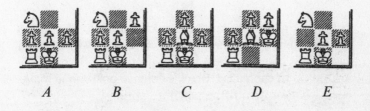

A   *B*   *C*   *D*   *E*

A is the normal position after king's side castling; *B* shows a slight weakening of the pawn structure, but against this there is now an escape square for the king off the back rank (remember the lesson of **59***A*!). *C* is strong but is weak without the bishop, as all the pawns are on dark squares which means that the light squares could be well used by the enemy (look back to **62***H*). *D* combines the ideas in *B* and *C*. *E* is good for attack (as the rook has an open line) but a little weaker for defence because there are only two pawns to shield the king.

74

A pawn in the centre is worth more than one at the side, at least during the main battle. From this you will understand that when you have a choice of pawns for a capture it is better to take with the one farthest from the middle because it will then be brought one file nearer. *A* and *B* show this.

| *A* | *B* | *C* | *D* | *E* |

Pawns in attack can be used to destroy the king's fortress and open lines for the pieces to work on. A sacrifice is often the best way to do this. *C, D* and *E* are examples. In each case, Black's defence position is weakened whether or not the pawn is captured.

75 *The Queen*

The pawns have claimed our attention so far. Let us now look at the pieces in turn and see how each can be used to best advantage.

The queen is at her best on an open board, especially when the enemy forces are scattered and unprotected. In the early part of the game the queen plays only a modest part, and that at a safe distance from the close fighting. The queen's weakness is that, being the best piece, she must move if attacked.

Do not bring the queen out too early for your opponent may then gain time by attacking her whilst developing his own pieces. Do not exchange your queen if you have the weaker force: she may later be able to worry the enemy king, for as we saw earlier the queen is the easiest piece with which to mate.

Rooks like *open files* to work on. Open files are files without pawns on them.

Rooks that are doubled on an open file can prove very strong, particularly if in the centre or near the enemy king. Make open files for your rooks by exchanging pawns. The rook does not work well on the ranks with one exception – the seventh rank, where the opponent's pawns stand at the start of a game. Here the rook is at its best for it can:

(*a*) Attack unmoved pawns, itself free from pawn attack;
(*b*) Confine the enemy king to the edge of the board.

In *A* you will see that a rook on the seventh can tie down enemy pieces to the defence of pawns. *B* shows one way of challenging this threat: if the white rook checks, the king moves up and Black's pawns are secure. *C–F* demonstrate the power of a rook on the seventh coupled with a discovered check – a marriage of the positional and the tactical. White uncovers a check with a capture, forcing the king to move (*D*) and then returns to drive the king into the corner (*E*) and repeat the slaughter (*F*). All Black's queen's side men are lost in this way, including the queen.

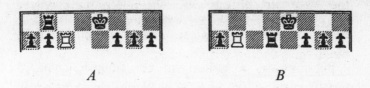

A   *B*

It is a good principle not to put your rook in front of your pawns, for here it will be open to attack and may also get in the way of a pawn which you wish to

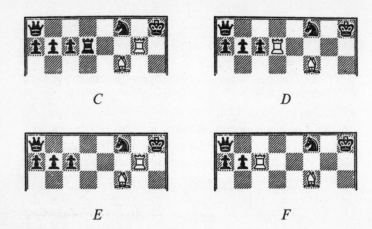

C

D

E

F

advance. The rook is a long-range piece and is best placed at the back of your army until later in the game or until it can be played with safety to the seventh rank.

77

The minor pieces are the real workers of the game. The bishop is active from the start but, like the major pieces, prefers open lines.

The peculiar feature of the bishop is its 'one-colour' move. A bishop's freedom is limited if 'friendly' pawns occupy many of the same-coloured squares: bishops are sometimes reduced to doing the work of pawns!

A shows a bishop on the same-coloured squares as the pawns. White controls less than half of the mini-board and black pieces can walk freely on the light squares.

By contrast, a bishop on the opposite-coloured squares has freedom of movement and works well with friendly pawns – compare *B*, where the white men control nearly twice as many squares.

It is common, for reasons we need not discuss, for a player in the course of a game to get most of his pawns

70

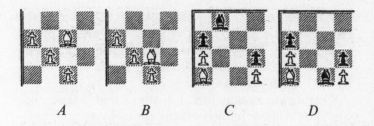

A   B   C   D

on the squares of one colour. It is also common for the
other player to have most of his pawns on the squares of
the opposite colour. The bishop that is then best for
defence (as in *B*) is also best for attack since it is on the
same colour as most of the opposing pawns. This is
called the *good bishop* and its companion the *bad bishop*.
C illustrates a good bishop (the white one) and a bad
bishop.

If you are left with a bad bishop, it is better to post it
in front of the pawns (*D*) rather than behind (*C*), for
here at least it has more space. A bad bishop, as in these
examples, is often tied to defence whilst a good bishop
can move about looking for targets and can also choose
the moment to attack them. This small study would be
of little importance if both sides kept both bishops
throughout a game, but this rarely happens. Each time a
bishop of either side can be exchanged you have to
consider whether it is, or will become, a good or bad
bishop, and act accordingly. These are easy words, and
on a crowded board and in the heat of the battle it is
easy to overlook this important positional factor.

78 *The Knights*

The knight, because of its short step and the ease with
which it can move on a crowded board, is most valuable
in the early and middle stages of a game when there are
many pawns about. As these are exchanged or captured
the long-moving pieces become stronger and the

knights, because of this, weaker. A knight posted in the centre where it is also free from attack by enemy pawns is very strong. Knights at the side of the board are weak because they attack fewer squares (22) and do not bear on the central position.

Knights are equally useful in attack and defence, but you should avoid moving them about looking for victims just because they have an interesting move or in the hope that their sly threats may be overlooked.

79 *The King*

The king must be kept in safety for most of the game. The best way to do this is to castle and then to make as few pawn moves in front of the king as necessary. King's-side castling is more common than queen's-side castling because it can be achieved quicker (there is one piece less to move off the back line) and because the king then defends the wing pawn which it does not on the queen's side. When most of the pieces have gone from the board and there is little risk of checkmate the king can come out of hiding. What is more, he can prove a very useful piece; for example, as a companion for a pawn marching towards promotion or as an executioner amongst the enemy pawns. At close range, a king is stronger than any other piece except the queen and he should be used to take advantage of this.

80 *Exchanging Men*

Several times we have talked about 'exchanging' – taking an enemy man for the loss of one of our men of equal value (a pawn for a pawn, a bishop for a knight). Opportunities for exchanging are likely to arise many times in a game and it is natural to ask whether it is good or bad to 'exchange'. The answer depends on the position.

A good first rule is that if you are ahead in material or under heavy attack you should try to exchange; if behind, or you are attacking, you should avoid exchanges, particularly of the queens.

Here are other things you should think about.

(a) Exchanges usually favour one side or the other, even if only slightly. Consider the men to be exchanged, particularly if a bishop is involved (77). Which man is better placed or is likely to become stronger (you have to think ahead here)?

(b) Will the position of a man that makes the recapture be better or worse afterwards?

(c) Will the exchange still be possible next move (it may be better to delay it)?

(d) Would it be in your favour if your opponent captured first, and if so, can you make him do so?

These questions are not too difficult to answer where the men to be exchanged are similar. It is much more difficult to decide whether a bishop should be exchanged for a knight, or perhaps a queen and pawn for two rooks. Here you need especially to consider the pieces' positional values which we have been discussing. These values, remember, take large account of the pawn structure.

81

Here now are two positions which we will discuss in general terms only.

White is a piece behind in *A* yet will win because of his big positional advantage. White has most space and is in command of the two open files. The white minor pieces are well placed and the advanced pawns cramp the black position. Notice how White controls all the dark-square 'holes' in the centre and on the king's side.

If you look closely at the black position you will see that no man can move without loss. This is an extreme case to show clearly what is meant by a 'positional advantage' – Black in fact is in 'zugzwang' (31).

A

B

By contrast, *B* is an ordinary position from an ordinary game. Let us make a quick assessment of this position. Black is a pawn ahead in material; has a well-placed knight in the centre which is secure from pawn attack; a queen's side pawn majority (making it easier to get a passed pawn on this side); a 'good' bishop, though inactive at present, and a safe king position. White's knight is also well placed; he has a good line of attack for his king's rook, and he is threatening either to break up the pawns on Black's queen's side or to get a rook to the seventh rank after exchanging pawns. Like Black, his king's position is safe at present. White is attacking but Black can also find interesting play – for example, by striking at White's central pawn. Verdict: a fairly level game, depending on whose turn it is to move.

Try to look at your games like this. In every position there are signposts that should give you ideas that will help you to find the right, or at least a good move. If you read only a few of these signposts your play will rapidly improve.

82 *Judgment*

You now have an insight into the elements of both tactical and positional play. However, if chess was only a matter of applying correctly the simple principles we have been looking at, it would be a dull game. But chess is never dull. At each move the players are faced with a new situation in which there will probably be several good, or good-looking moves, positional or tactical or both. So at each turn the players must make a decision – which move is best? This is the hardest part of the game – we call it *judgment*. Sound judgment comes with experience. In your games you should try to see one or two moves ahead in those lines of play you think are important (not every line: you would need a computer to do that!).

Looking ahead means not only planning your own moves but also foreseeing the moves your opponent may make in reply. Do not spend much time on this. It is usually better not to attempt to work out moves accurately except where you think a combination is forced; that is, where one or both sides must follow a certain line of play to avoid loss. Instead, try to look at your game as we examined the positions above – in general terms only. This should help you find a plan and from it your move. Anyone who says 'I don't know what to do now' (and someone is always saying it!) is just not thinking.

PART FOUR

Scoring

83
Notations

It is a feature of chess that games and positions can be simply and briefly recorded. This is of great value for it means that we can learn from and enjoy the games of the experts and also keep a record of our own games. A record of a game is called a *game score* or simply a *score*.

There are several scoring systems, or *notations* as they are usually called, but only three are common. The ALGEBRAIC and the DESCRIPTIVE are used for recording games whilst the FORSYTH is used for recording positions. The Algebraic is in general use. The Descriptive is falling from favour but is standard in old books.

When studied for the first time these systems may seem difficult and confusing, but they are really neither and you will be surprised how quickly you are able to use them.

84
We will examine the Algebraic and Descriptive notations together for they have much in common. If you later want to keep a record of your games you can then decide which system you prefer. The Algebraic will be used for the rest of this book.

85
Notations describe chess moves accurately and as briefly as possible. The elements of a move are two:

(*a*) The man moved;
(*b*) The square to which the man is moved.

It is enough to record these: there is normally no need to describe also the square on which the man stands before the move.

Both the Algebraic and the Descriptive identify the men by initial letters:

K – king	Q – queen	R – rook
B – bishop	N or Kt – knight	P – pawn

(A further economy is practised in the Algebraic: the P initial is dropped, it being understood that a move which is not prefixed by a capital letter is a pawn move. Symbols, as used in diagrams, now frequently replace initial letters in books and magazines.)

The two systems differ, however, in their description of the squares.

86

In the Algebraic notation the files of the chessboard are lettered 'a' to 'h' from left to right and the ranks from 1 to 8 from bottom to top *as seen from White's side of the board*. A square is described by its file and rank designation in that order. For example, the bottom left square is a1 (see diagram overleaf). Note that each square has a unique description.

In the Descriptive notation, the *files are named after the pieces standing on them in the initial position*. Pieces on the king's side are called after the king (king's rook, king's knight, king's bishop) and those on the queen's side are similarly called after the queen. Notice that the file descriptions are the same for White and Black. The ranks are numbered 1 to 8 *from each side*. White's second rank, for example, is Black's seventh rank (see diagram overleaf).

A square is described by file and rank, in that order. So each square has two names, one read from the White side of the board and the other from the Black side (it may help you to turn the diagram round to see this).

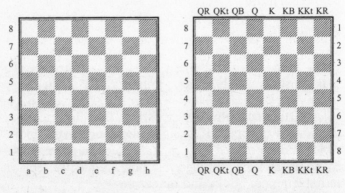

ALGEBRAIC NOTATION   DESCRIPTIVE NOTATION

White's K1, for example, is Black's K8; White's QKt4 is the same square as Black's QKt5, and so on. Notice again that the file description is the same for both sides and that the sum of the ranks reckoned from each side adds up to nine (thus your third rank is your opponent's sixth, etc.).

87

A move is recorded in both systems by the symbol for the man moved, followed by a hyphen (usually omitted in the Algebraic) and the symbol for the square to which the move is made. In the Descriptive notation *a White move is always recorded from White's side of the board and a Black move from Black's side of the board*. Let us suppose that both players move their kings one square up the file from the initial position. Both White and Black moves would be described as K–K2 in the Descriptive notation and would be written down like this by both players; in the Algebraic notation, the White move would be described as Ke2 and the Black move as Ke7 and both players would write the moves down in this way.

88

Notation is chess shorthand, and like shorthand it should be as brief and clear as possible. Often two similar men of the same colour can move to the same square, so it is necessary to indicate which man is moved. This is done in the Algebraic by indicating *either* the rank *or* the file on which the man stands. For example, if you had a rook on a1 and the other on a3, and you wanted to move the one in the corner to a2, the move would be described as R1a2. If you had rooks on a1 and c1 and you wanted to move the one in the corner to b1, the move would be recorded as Rab1. With rooks on a1 and c3 and you wished to advance the corner rook to a3, you could record this either as Raa3 or as R1a3. Look back to (**74A** and B) for an example of a pawn capture. This would be recorded as axb3.

With the Descriptive notation, the same principle is applied: the square on which the piece stands is indicated immediately after the piece symbol. See diagram D in (90) for an example.

89 *Notation Symbols*

A capture is shown in both notations by an 'x' (sometimes, in the Algebraic only, by a colon). This is followed in the Algebraic by the square on which the capture is made and in the Descriptive by the symbol for the man captured.

Other symbols used in one or both notations are given overleaf.

Symbol	Meaning
– (hyphen)	to
x (or):	takes
+ (or) ch	check
‡ (or) mate	checkmate
(Q) (or)	Promotion to
(= Q)	queen (after pawn move)
dis ch	discovered check
dbl ch	double check
0–0 (or)	Castles
Castles (K)	king's side
0–0–0 (or)	Castles
Castles (Q)	queen's side
ep	en passant
!	good move
?	bad move
!?	move that may be good or bad

90

Below is the end of a game, shown move by move, in which both the Algebraic (in **bold** type) and Descriptive notations are used for comparison. All the types of moves that may give difficulty in scoring are included. Also, the game is a good example of complicated tactical play. Comments cover both recording of moves and the purpose of the moves in the game.

A – Black is to play in this position. White is threatening to win a rook for nothing by moving the knight away to give a discovered check.

B – Black moves the queen. Notice that Q–B2 would not be a sufficient description as the queen could also have moved to QB2. Now White has no discovered check and Black is attacking the bishop with his queen.

A – Black to Play

(Black Moves)
B – **Qf7** Q–KB2

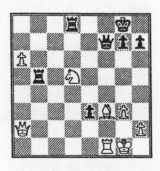

(White Moves)
C – **0–0** Castles

(Black Moves)
D – **Rbxd5**
R(Kt4)xKt

C – White defends the bishop by castling. This move would only be allowed if the king and rook had not moved previously. White is now in a position to uncover an attack on the queen by moving the bishop.

D – Black captures the knight with a rook, hoping to win two minor pieces for a rook. As the capture could have been made by either black rook, you should note carefully how the move is recorded in each notation.

E – White surprisingly does not recapture the rook but plays on the pawn which is now only one square off promotion. Only one pawn can move to R7, so there is no need to describe this move as 'P–QR7'.

(White Moves)
E – **a7** P–R7

(Black Moves)
F – **e2** P–K7

F – Black counter-attacks, threatening the white rook.

(White Moves)
G – **Bxe2** BxP

(Black Moves)
H – **Rf5** R–KB4

G – White could easily have made a bad move here: if he had taken the pawn with the queen instead of with

the bishop, Black would have been able to capture
White's advanced pawn with a check (look at this – it is
not easy to see). Calamitous for White would have been
Bxd5 (instead of Bxe2) when Black would have had the
crushing reply exf1(Q) mate. Instead of the move
played, White could also have won with the clever
sacrifice Qxd5!

H – As this rook can move also to QB4, the description 'R–B4' is not sufficient. Notice the black queen is
now pinned and the white queen is 'en prise'.

(White Moves)

I – **a8(Q)** P–R8 (=Q)

(Black Moves)

J – **Rxf1+** RxRch

I – White promotes the pawn and now has two queens
on the board (a rook can be turned upside down to
represent a second queen during a game).

J – Here, as in *D* and *G*, the Descriptive notation
shows the man captured, and the Algebraic the square
on which the capture is made.

(White Moves)
K – **Bxf1** BxR

(Black Moves)
L – **Rxa8** RxQ

(White Moves)
M – **Qxa8+** QxRch

(Black Moves)
N – **Qf8** Q–B1

O – In the Descriptive notation when a side has only one bishop left, the simple move description 'B–B4' is always correct since the bishop could never play to KB4 and QB4 or any other matched pair of squares as these are always of opposite colours. Discovery of chessboard facts like this will widen your understanding and help you to play the game better.

(White Moves)   (Black Moves)

O – **Bc4+** B–B4ch   *P* – **Kh8** K–R1

P – The king has been forced away from protection of the queen which is again pinned. A 'back rank' mate, such as we saw in **62*B*** follows.

(White Moves)

Q – **Qxf8 mate** QxQ mate

91   *Forsyth Notation*

The FORSYTH is a quick and accurate way of recording positions (useful, for example, when a game has to be broken off). Unoccupied squares are indicated by the appropriate number and the men by the usual abbreviations, capital letters for the white men and small letters for the black men.

Starting at the top left of the chessboard seen from White's side (square a8) each rank in turn is recorded from left to right, ending with the bottom right-hand square (h1). Ranks are divided by strokes but two or more empty ranks may be grouped together. Chessmen and square numbers should of course add up to 64! The final position above (*Q*) would be recorded in Forsyth as:

5Q1k/6pp/16/2B5/6P1/7P/6K1

PART FIVE

Playing the Game

92

You now have a fair idea of the peculiarities of the different men and how they behave in attack and defence, and you also know the differences between positional and tactical play. Before we begin a proper game, however, we need to know how to apply our knowledge so that our moves may have purpose from the start.

93

Let us follow a game through in outline without making moves. At the beginning, only the knights and pawns can move so our first task is to give our other pieces freedom and then to get them on to good squares for both attack and defence. A good square may be described as one on which a man is well placed to take part in the coming battle, and where he has *mobility*, or freedom of movement. A man's mobility may be limited by enemy men who oppose it or by friendly men who get in its way, or both. A good square for one man (a knight, for example) will probably be a bad square for another man (say a rook) because different men command different squares. This early part of the game, when the first task of each side is to 'get the pieces out' or *develop* them (both terms are well used) is called the OPENING. The next stage, that of the battle proper, is known as the MIDDLE GAME. There is no clear division between the opening and the middle game.

94

In the middle game, your plans should be directed towards making and attacking weak points in your opponent's position and avoiding or defending weaknesses in your own position. Each move you make is therefore either an attacking move or a defensive move, or often a move that is part attacking, part defensive. An attacking move is often the best defensive move anyway because in chess, as in many other games, attack is one of the best forms of defence. If you become a good chessplayer you will find that there is never time for an idle and pointless move.

95

After the middle game, when the big battle has died down, comes the END GAME. In the end game, the kings are usually out of direct danger because there are fewer men left on the board. Pawn promotion is often the main aim of each side in an end game. Opening, middle game and end game are merely terms used to describe three different stages of the game, but a game of chess remains a whole – a single, continuous fight from start to finish.

96

We are now ready to play through the score of an actual game. The moves of a game are numbered progressively and each number covers a move by both players. If we wish to talk about a particular move it is necessary to state who made it; for example, White's seventh move, Black's eighteenth.

The game given is between strong players and contains many examples of play that we have studied. Follow the game through on a board and check with the diagrams that you are doing this correctly. Set up the men in the initial position (5) – dark squares left-hand corner, remember! White always moves first.

	WHITE	BLACK
1.	e4	c6
2.	d4	d5
3.	exd5	cxd5

Both players have been fighting for control of the centre which is for the moment shared. It is also locked – neither central pawn can move.

4.	c4

The opening is given its character by this move. An expert will tell you that this is the Panov–Botvinnik attack in the Caro–Kann defence – chess often sounds more difficult than it is!

4.	...	Nf6
5.	Nc3	e6
6.	Nf3	Nc6

Both players activate their unmoved knights.

7.	Bd3	dxc4
8.	Bxc4	Be7

Some interesting things have been happening. After White had developed his king's bishop, Black exchanged pawns, making White move the bishop again. White could not long delay moving this bishop because he needs to castle, but equally he did not want himself to

| Position after Black's | Position after White's |
| 8th move | 11th move |

exchange pawns, perhaps because he saw it would free
the black queen's bishop which is at present shut in and
lacks mobility. Now White has an isolated pawn in the
centre, but since it is on the fourth rank whilst Black's
centre pawn is on the third and cannot advance to the
fourth without loss, White has more space in the centre
to make up for the isolation of his pawn. The plans of
both sides are based on this central pawn position.
Black will play to bring his forces to attack the isolated
pawn which he hopes will prove a weakness to White,
whilst his opponent intends to make use of his greater
freedom in the middle and the fact that Black's QB is
shut in to prepare an attack against the king. Both sides
are continuing to develop their pieces. Check your position now with the diagram.

9.	0–0	0–0
10.	Re1	a6

Black's last move is a common manoeuvre. He
prepares to advance his b-pawn gaining space on the
queen's side, forcing the white bishop to move again
and also allowing the black bishop to get to b7 where

it will bear down on the light-coloured squares in the centre. White's next move is the usual counter to this idea (check your position against the diagram). Let us see what might then happen if Black continued with his plan (this is not part of the game remember!) 11. a4, b5?; 12. axb5, axb5?; 13. Rxa8, and White is winning.

| 11. | a4 | Qd6 |
| 12. | Be3 | Rd8 |

The threat to White's isolated centre pawn is building up. Black has three pieces attacking it now: notice that the rook behind the queen is one of these although it does not directly threaten the pawn.

| 13. | Qe2 | Bd7 |
| 14. | Rad1 | |

Now, suddenly, White has achieved an almost ideal position; all his pieces bear on the centre and are on good squares and the king is in safety. The black pieces are not so happy. The two bishops are lazy and the queen is awkwardly placed. Black suffers from too little room to move about so that his pieces are in one another's way. White has gained in space. However, Black's disadvantage may only prove temporary and at present he has no permanent weaknesses in his position (see diagram on page 93).

| 14. | ... | Nb4 |

As the white d-pawn is isolated, d5 is an ideal square for a knight, as we have seen (78). Black plans to take advantage of this but if he moves the KKt at once to d5, White will be able to exchange it and Black will be obliged to retake with the pawn when he will have failed in his aim of achieving a positional strong-point. The move played will allow him to secure a knight at d5.

15.   Ne5

White's knight moves directly to a good central square and also frees the f-pawn to advance if necessary.

15.   ...   Nbd5
16.   Nxd5   Nxd5
17.   Qh5

Now White starts the attack on the king's position and threatens to take off the bishop's pawn which is twice attacked (by the knight and the queen) and only once defended (by the king). Notice that White could not have played his last move if he had not exchanged knights the move before as the black knight was guarding the square the white queen now occupies. White does not wish to exchange his bishop for the remaining black knight as he plans to use it to attack the light-coloured squares around the enemy king.

17.   ...   Be8
18.   Bd3

The black bishop has been forced back in defence and now White threatens to checkmate in two moves. (Can you see this? If Black does not take action, White will play Qxh7+ followed by Qh8 mate.) This is not the purpose of White's move however, for he cannot expect his opponent to overlook the danger. The plan involves the sacrifice of a pawn which will signal an all-out attack on the black king.

18.   ...   Nf6

Position after White's
14th move

Position after White's
17th move

It may surprise you that this strong-looking move probably loses the game. Correct was 18... f5; uncovering an attack on the queen and shutting out the dangerous white bishop.

19.   Qh4   Bxa4

The white queen would be attacked if the black knight moved – a 'discovered attack' – but she is safe for the moment as a knight move would allow either the mate mentioned above or the capture of the knight by the queen. Look at each of the five possible moves by this knight and satisfy yourself that this is correct.

Black decides to take the pawn White has sacrificed, but this loses an important tempo and removes one of the only two pieces defending the king. Black now has two pawns to one on the queen's side and hopes to win in the end game after stopping the attack on his king.

20.   Rd2   Bb5
21.   Bb1   g6

Some more interesting play. Black was prepared, on his 20th move, to allow his extra pawn to be doubled and isolated in order to get rid of the white bishop, but White wisely keeps the piece by moving it away.

Black now tries to block the attack by moving up his g-pawn, but this creates a weakness on the dark squares round the king (compare **59D**). Now White's other bishop becomes dangerous as a result. Black could have stopped White's next move by 21... h6 (instead of 21... g6) but then White would have had the bright sacrifice 22. Bxh6!, breaking open the defence.

If Black then accepted the sacrifice (22... gxh6) White would have continued 23. Qxh6!, and since the black knight would still have been unable to move because of the mate starting with Qh7+, there would have been no good answer to the White threat of Re3 followed by Rg3. You are probably bewildered by these possibilities, but it is enough if you have noticed how weak a king who has lost his pawn defence can be.

22.   Bg5   Nd5

Position after Black's   Position after Black's
19th move   22nd move

The white move attacked the knight twice and it was only once defended. Black moves the knight so that the bishop is defended twice (necessary, as it is now twice attacked). However, the knight has been forced away from the defence of the king's position where White now has several pieces concentrated: White is ready to strike! Black could have defended the knight instead of moving it by the move 22... Kg7; but this would also have lost although the play is rather too complicated to go into here.

| 23. | Nxf7 | Kxf7 |
| 24. | Qxh7+ | Ke8 |

Black had to take the offered knight. If instead he had tried 23... Bxg5; White would have continued 24. Nxg5 and there would have been two white pieces attacking both the rook's pawn and the king's pawn, each of which would have been only once defended – a double attack which could not have been met. White would then have been a pawn ahead in material and the black king without shelter – a hopeless situation in a game between strong players.

| 25. | Bxg6+ | Kd7 |
| 26. | Rxe6! | |

Another sacrifice! White now has three pawns for the knight and so is level in material, but Black is desperately placed. He cannot take the rook with either king or queen. Notice 26... Kxe6? 27. Bf5, a curious mid-board checkmate. Also after 26... Qxe6; again 27. Bf5 and the black queen is pinned and lost for the bishop. After this exchange (queen for bishop) the point count on each side would be White 22, Black 21. Only a one-point advantage, but White would control most space, the black pieces would be tied to the defence of the king – a real danger of checkmate exists in this sort of position – and White would probably be able to promote one of his king's-side pawns without difficulty.

| 26. | ... | Qb4 |
| 27. | Bf5 | Kc7 |

Black must escape the terrible 'discovered check' that is threatened (see **44**).

| 28. | Bxe7 | Qxd2 |

Black allows a discovered check. He could have retaken the bishop with the knight (28... Nxe7) but after White's 29. Rxe7+, the end would not have been far off. Follow through this possible finish: 28... Nxe7 (instead of 28... Qxd2); 29. Rxe7+, Kb6; 30. Rxb7+, Ka5; 31. Qc7+, Ka4; 32. Bc2+, Qb3; 33. Qc3 and White will mate next move however Black plays. (Work this out: not all the replies are easy to see.) This is a good example of what is called a 'king hunt'. However, these are all dreams, for Black decided to take the unguarded White rook. You can recover the game position from the diagram.

Position after White's
26th move

Final position

| 29. | Bd6 dbl ch | |

96

At this point Black gives up the game. Because White's last move was a double check, the black king would have to move. He has three squares to choose from; let's see what would then happen in each case.

(*a*) 29... Kc6; 30. Bc5 dis ch, Rd6; 31. Rxd6 mate.

(*b*) 29... Kc8; 30. Re8 dis ch, Bd7; 31. Q (or B) xd7 mate.

(*c*) 29... Kb6 (best); 30. Bb4 dis ch, Bc6; 31. Bxd2, and now Black, nine points behind in material, is soon lost.

97

Of course this game was difficult for you to follow and you will not be able to think and play like this for a long time. The game was an exciting one though, and did show clearly several useful things: the early fight for the centre and how the plans of each side grew from it, an attack on the king's position where the attacking force was better placed and stronger than the defending force, the sacrifice to break down the pawn defence and the king chase that followed. The game did not reach an end game proper for there were still many pieces on the board at the surrender.

98

When you yourself start playing you will make many mistakes – not just little mistakes (you will make these most of the time!) but big mistakes, like putting your queen 'en prise' or allowing your king to be mated when you are not looking. You will make big positional mistakes too, though they will not be so obvious. But all these mistakes will be steps to knowledge and you will soon find that you make fewer and fewer bad mistakes and you will then be able to pay more attention to the smaller mistakes. Win or lose, though, the game is the thing – and if you forget that chess is a game it is better to forget chess.

99 *Planning*

When you play chess, always have a plan. At the start of a game, your plan will probably be to get your pieces on to good squares and, if possible, to capture the centre. Be ready to change your plan, however, if your opponent makes what you think is a bad mistake. In the middle game you may develop a bold plan, such as a direct attack on the king as White carried out in the above game, or a less ambitious and perhaps better plan of securing some positional advantage – a rook on the seventh rank perhaps, a well-posted knight or a strong pawn centre. At each move you will have to consider whether your plan is still the best one – this is where judgment comes in. Do not be afraid to change your plan – in fact, you will need to change it, perhaps many times in the course of a game. A plan is based on the position and takes account of all the men on both sides. Do not be tempted to make a move which is not part of your plan unless you think the move is necessary. It is a common failing to make a move that is not part of a general plan, and perhaps is even without reason. At best, such moves are wasted but more often they are simply bad.

100 *Resigning*

In conclusion, let us see the various ways in which a game can end. We have already met three: checkmate, stalemate, and by surrender, as in the above game. We talk of the player who gives up as RESIGNING the game. It is right to resign a game in which no chance remains for this saves time and is also polite. However, what makes up a hopeless position will depend on the strength of the players and it is best, when starting to play, to carry on until checkmate. Another way to end the game has nothing to do with the position on the board. When a time limit is set on the number of moves that each side must make, and this is usual in match play, then a player who oversteps this limit loses the game.

101 *Drawn Game*

In the same way that one player can resign, so can both players agree a DRAW at any time during the game; one player offers, the other accepts and the game is over. This is the usual manner in which a draw is reached but there are several other ways.

(a) Insufficient Force

Neither side is strong enough to force mate. An obvious example is where each side is left with just a king. This will be explained more fully later.

(b) Perpetual Check

A position is sometimes reached where one side can force a continuous series of checks – a sort of see-saw or merry-go-round. Here are three examples:

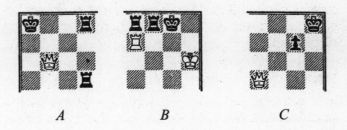

A   B   C

In *A*, after 1. Qa6+, Kb8; 2. Qb6+, Kc8; 3. Qc6+, the king must go back again. In *B*, play could go 1. Rg7+, Kh8; 2. Rh7+, Kg8; for ever. In *C*, after 1. Qe8+, Kh7; 2. Qh5+, Kg8; these moves can be repeated indefinitely.

White could equally have played 1. Qh5+, for the same result. A player who is otherwise losing will be happy to force a perpetual check; a player who is winning will seek to avoid it.

(c) *Repeated Position*

If the identical position occurs three times in a game with the same player to move, a draw may be claimed by either player. A perpetual check is one kind of repeated position.

(d) *Fifty-move Rule*

This is a very rare finish. Where both sides have made fifty consecutive moves without a pawn being played or a capture made, either side may claim a draw. In certain specified positions, the number of moves is increased.

PART SIX

The Openings

102

We have seen that a game of chess always starts from the same position, known as the *initial position*. The first moves of both sides are known as the OPENINGS. The openings are established sequences of moves for both sides that are considered to be the best, or at least playable in the sense that no early disaster will befall players who adhere to them. Today opening play between top players can easily run to 20 moves or more a side where both players are following a recognized line. Established openings have been developed through play between masters of the game and through analysis, or commonly a combination of both. Openings have names, often exotic names, as do many of the variations of standard openings. Names are meaningful to regular players and are necessary for reference. A great number of books have been written about the openings, but with a tendency to date as improvements are discovered. These books are aimed at experienced players and will have little value for you at present.

103

Learning openings, in the sense of committing to memory sequences of moves, is however not recommended for the recreational player. It is better to try and absorb the basic ideas; the best squares for the pieces, what you are trying to achieve, and so on. Bearing in mind that White, at the start of a game, has a choice of no fewer than 20 moves of which perhaps eight can be considered good to reasonable, and Black has an equal number of replies, it can be seen that after a few moves the number of playable lines is beginning to approach the astronomical. Our knowledge of the openings is constantly advancing as old lines are revitalised and new lines are explored. Also openings, like hemlines, tend to go in and out of fashion.

Do not be intimidated at the prospect: more than one world champion has been noted for his deficiencies in this stage of the game. A former British champion, whom we shall call X, was renowned for his lack of opening knowledge. One day he was playing Y, also a former British champion and an opening buff. X surprised Y with a move recommended by the Russians (who are rather good at chess) in analysis that had reached Y only a day or two previously. How could X have known about it? He had not: asked after the game, our opening cripple replied, 'I never seriously considered any other move.'

That points up the lesson that if you play according to sound principles, you are likely to follow the approved openings whether you know them or not.

This is not to decry opening knowledge. Other things being equal, the player who is better versed in the openings is at an advantage. However, parrot learning of opening moves (everyone deplores it; everyone does it) is to be avoided as far as possible, particularly at this undistinguished stage in your chess career. There is no merit in playing your first ten, carefully rehearsed, moves like Kramnik or Kasparov if, on your eleventh move, your memory exhausted, you play like King Kong.

104

We will take the openings slowly but, before we start *Sudden Death* a couple of horror scenarios are not out of place.

Defeat can come quickly in the opening if you sin against principles. The shortest game of chess is only two moves long and is known, rather unfairly as it is not obvious, as Fool's Mate. White ignores the centre and development and instead moves wing pawns that bare his king.

	WHITE	BLACK
1.	g4	e5 (or e6)
2.	f3 (or f4)	Qh4 mate

There is an attack much favoured by beginners that can also come to a quick end. This example is known as Scholar's Mate.

	WHITE	BLACK
1.	e4	e5
2.	Bc4	Bc5
3.	Qf3 (or h5)	Nc6
4.	Qxf7 mate	

Game 1: Final Position

Game 2: Final Position

White's play, although successful here, was not good because the queen was brought out too early, which is a positional mistake (**75**). Also, the attack relied on Black overlooking the threat to the bishop's pawn (he could have played 3... Qe7). Do not make a move or a combination whose success depends on your opponent not seeing your plan: this is bad chess. It is certain that you will face several attempts to bluff you with this attack so make sure you understand how to defend against it.

105 *Main Aims*

It would be nice if we could reduce all the openings to a few general rules of play; this however is not possible, for whilst some openings are straightforward, others are hugely difficult. Again, some offer plenty of tactical play, even in the first few moves, others little or none. But there are a few features that are common to most openings and these deserve our special study. Two aims stand out from the rest: to get one's pieces on to good squares and to strike at the centre. We have already explained their importance. If you follow these guides alone you will not play the openings badly.

You will have absorbed a number of useful principles, a lot of sound ideas, and you will have improved your game to the point where you can think about taking up a proper study of the openings. If you want to, that is. If not, then at least you will be equipped to handle the opening with some confidence and have the experience to deal with new situations. That should give you the advantage over most casual players. Hereon you will find it useful to have a chess set with the men arranged in the starting position. The diagrams show the board either from White's or Black's standpoint according to the moves under discussion. It is always wise to consider a position from both sides of the board. Let us begin by looking at the first move, good or bad, by each player.

106 *Move One, and a Dose of Theory*

Hereon in our study of the openings full-board diagrams are numbered for ease of reference. Be careful not to confuse these numbers with those of the sections which are always in **bold**. You know the starting position (*1*).

BLACK

WHITE

1

There is no known way in which one side can force an advantage. If there were, there would be no chess openings and probably no game called chess. This position is as baffling today as it has always been.

There are 20 possible opening moves for White. Of these, two are more popular than all the others combined. Most chess games, whether between modest players, experts or masters, are opened by moving up one of the central pawns, thus:

WHITE   WHITE

2   3

That does not mean that other moves are inferior. Here are two good opening moves that are by no means uncommon:

BLACK   BLACK

WHITE   WHITE

4   5

Certain other moves, though less often played, also have their merits. Here are two:

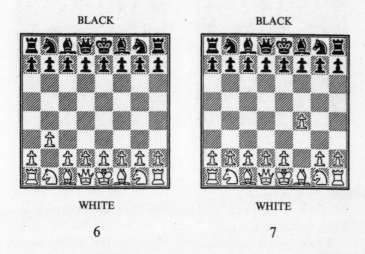

6   7

On the other hand, some opening moves are to be condemned as downright bad. Here are four:

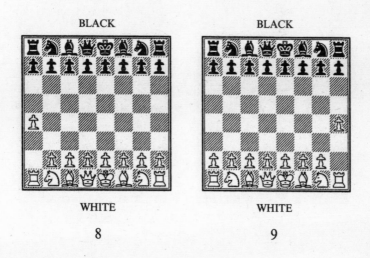

8   9

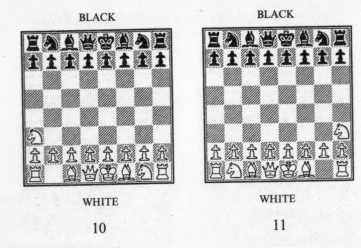

BLACK

BLACK

WHITE

WHITE

10

11

The first move of a chess game carries no threats. It follows that Black has a variety of options for his reply.

Again, some are recognized as better than others while some are simply more popular than others. Let us consider plausible responses to the usual opening moves (2) and (3). In both cases, an excellent course for Black is to respond in the same way:

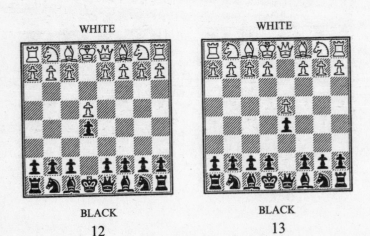

WHITE

WHITE

BLACK

BLACK

12

13

Other good responses to (2) are the following:

WHITE

BLACK

14

WHITE

BLACK

15

Several others are perfectly playable:

WHITE

BLACK

16

WHITE

BLACK

17

WHITE

BLACK

18

WHITE

BLACK

19

WHITE

BLACK

20

Other good responses to (*3*) are:

WHITE

BLACK

21

WHITE

BLACK

22

WHITE

BLACK

23

WHITE

BLACK

24

Notice that in (*24*) Black immediately offers a pawn to be taken. We will discuss this later.

Against each of the White opening moves (*4*) – (*7*) above, Black also has a choice of good responses.

However White opens, and however Black responds, White on his second turn will again have a choice of good moves. But before we progress further we must pause for a bit of theory.

The first move is a definite advantage. This fact determines the general objectives of both sides in the early stages of a game: White must strive to keep the advantage and must therefore play aggressively while Black will be seeking equality and will need to establish a cautious balance between defensive play and counter-attack. Of course, if Black is able to seize the initiative because of weak play by White, he will forget about equality and go over to the offensive.

Experts disagree about chess openings as experts are wont to disagree about everything. Nevertheless, certain strategic principles are not disputed, and of these two are paramount:

(i) Get your pieces into play as soon as possible;
(ii) Direct your play towards the centre of the board.

Developing your pieces ('developing' is the jargon word) means placing them on squares where they are effective for attack or defence and preferably both. In the starting position, the only pieces (as distinct from pawns) that can move are the knights. It is necessary to move at least two pawns before you can develop all the other pieces. What are the problems of development? Two, principally: your own pawns, which have a habit of getting in the way, and your opponent, who is not enthusiastic about your pieces occupying strong points and is likely to take such measures as he is able to stop them doing so.

Why direct your play towards the centre, and what is the centre anyway? The centre is important because it confers flexibility. A piece at the side of the board usually commands fewer squares than one in the centre and cannot be moved so easily to other parts of the board. It is therefore less effective.

The centre can be defined as the four central squares and, loosely, the twelve squares immediately around them (25). We saw this on page 13.

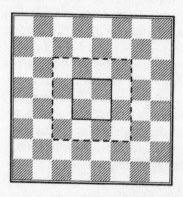

25

Let us now look at the moves above (2) – (24) in the light of these cardinal principles.

Moves (2) and (3) are admirable. They occupy central squares and at the same time allow bishop and queen to develop. Move (4) also strikes at the centre and frees the queen. Move (5) is a developing move, placing the knight on an ideal square to influence the central battle.

Notice that it is the king's knight (the knight on the king's side of the board). There is a good reason for this. The move assists preparation for castling on the king's side. The king is vulnerable in the middle and another opening principle is that he should be moved to safety before the main battle. This usually means castling, whereby a rook is simultaneously brought into play. Castling is both a protective and a developing move.

Castling on the king's side is favoured, for two reasons: it is easier to accomplish (one fewer piece to move out of the way) and, after castling, the rook's pawn (the pawn at the edge of the board) is guarded by the king, which it is not when castling queen's side.

Move (6) is harder to understand. It forms a redoubt for the bishop which will advance to the square vacated by the pawn. Here the piece will strike at the centre, protected from pawn attack. Thus the move meets our two criteria, if indirectly. It is therefore rather passive.

That is not to condemn it: it is part of an opening system. A system is a co-ordinated series of moves governed by strategic ideas. Development should not be at random but part of a general plan in which the pawns and pieces not only work to achieve their objectives, but also co-operate with and complement one another. There is nothing complex about this: all received openings are systems and these systems are likely to have long-term goals, like attacking on the king's side, securing the better pawn formation, exchanging off a powerful enemy bishop, and so forth. Do not let these trouble you at present.

Move (7) is a reflection of move (4) but carries a small element of risk since it opens lines near the king. Notice that if White had advanced this pawn only one square, the move would be thoroughly bad since it would carry the same element of risk but would not hit at the centre and would take away the best square for development of the knight.

It should now be clear why moves (8) – (11) are bad. They do not influence the centre and, in the case of (10) and (11), the knights are badly placed for both attack and defence. Beginners sometimes favour (8) and (9) as the simplest way of getting the rooks into play. This idea is mistaken; rooks do not belong in front of pawns where they are very vulnerable to attack.

Black's responses to White's opening moves need not detain us long.

114

It should be obvious why (*12*), (*13*) and (*14*) are good. Move (*15*) appears passive – although it releases one bishop, it shuts the door on the second one – but again this is the case of a system, which we will examine later.

Recall that Black must be careful in the early stages and this cautious approach is also reflected in (*16*) and (*18*). Move (*20*) on the other hand is instant aggression and although it is quite playable, it is not a favourite of the experts. You can probably deduce why.

The other Black replies need no comment, and you should not be in need of any more horrid examples – you can work out a few defective Black responses for yourself.

107

A Cautionary Interlude

We will now return to the board for a minute or two to look at a couple of ideas.

BLACK

WHITE

26

BLACK

WHITE

27

Suppose that after the opening moves (*20*) White decides to develop his bishop and at the same time give check (*26*). Is this a good idea? It is not. Checks are sometimes useful, sometimes useless. This one is rather worse than useless. Black replies as in (27) and now White must move the bishop again as it is attacked.

Where can he move it to? If he doesn't want to lose the pawn (pawns are valuable and should not be surrendered lightly, particularly pawns in the centre), he must play as in (28). Notice how the bishop's role is now reduced to that of a pawn, and further, the piece blocks the advance of the queen's pawn, adding to White's problems.

You may argue that Black's second move took away the best square from his knight even though it opened a line for the queen. Quite true, but in chess, as in life, it is rare to get something for nothing – be content, as Black would be here, that you are getting the better of the bargain.

Black seizes the centre by occupation (29) – notice that both his bishops are thereby released into play.

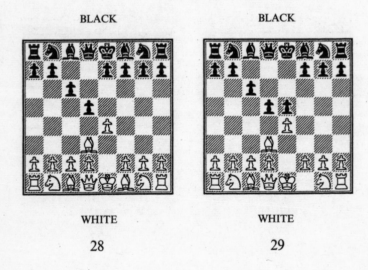

BLACK

BLACK

WHITE

WHITE

28

29

How is White to continue? Logically, he will want to get his king's knight developed sooner rather than later since he will be anxious to get his king to safety – it

WHITE

30

WHITE

31

WHITE

32

WHITE

33

would take him at least four moves before he could think about castling on the queen's side.

So he tries (30), which attacks a pawn. Black now forces the win of bishop or knight for pawn with the

sequence shown in *(31)* – *(35)*. This pawn fork of two minor pieces is quite a common theme in the openings. It occurs most often in the middle of the board. Be on your guard against it!

Another idea for White: why not exploit the advantage of the first move by bringing out the queen – the most powerful piece on the board – to bludgeon the black king? This manoeuvre is the novice's delight, the curtain-raiser of untold billions of games, but please reserve your applause.

Following from *(12)* (page 108), White develops a bishop where it bears down on Black's king position at the same time assisting preparations for castling *(36)*. A good idea? Certainly: faultless play so far.

Black responds, let us say (since he has other satisfactory moves), as in *(37)*, a sound developing play.

Now White advances his queen, threatening to checkmate Black *(38)*. Black easily parries the threat *(39)* when the position of White's queen proves something of an embarrassment. It is occupying the square wanted

36   37

for the king's knight and may later be attacked with advantage by the enemy queen's knight or, after Black moves his queen's pawn, by the bishop. Black has the initiative.

38   39

What have we learnt from these abortive ideas? A lesson that is valid for all opening play. Avoid attacks where the defence has an adequate resource and your pieces can be driven back with loss of time, or where they are left stranded on bad squares from which they must be moved, again with loss of time. Attacking moves with the queen in the opening sometimes work; but mostly they don't. The queen is best left indoors for a bit since she is particularly vulnerable to attack. The time to bring the queen out is when there are weaknesses in the enemy position of which advantage can be taken.

It is tempting to make attacking moves that depend on your opponent overlooking an obvious threat and in this way you may sometimes win games. If that pleases you, go ahead, but don't waste time reading further – this book is about improving your chess.

108 *Pawns are Important*

Many chessplayers (though none who are any good) look on pawns as something of a nuisance, particularly in the opening where, as we have observed, they can get in the way of piece development. After all, isn't the object of the game to checkmate the enemy king? And doesn't that mean attacking with your pieces?

We have seen that pawns are moved in the opening for two main reasons; to allow the pieces to come into play and to contest the centre. Pawns have other uses, too. They are ideal to spearhead an attack and to serve as a shield in defence. Nor is that all. Squares attacked by your pawns are unlikely to find favour with your opponent as resting places for his pieces – nobody likes giving up a piece for a paltry pawn. And that leads to the idea of sometimes posting pawns specifically to inhibit enemy pieces from occupying strong posts.

For example, quite often as a game develops, one or both sides advance a wing pawn, or even both pawns, one square. This is illustrated in (*40*) and (*41*). Ignore the other pawns and pieces for a moment. These moves are basically defensive and are usually employed when it is deemed necessary to stop a bishop pinning a knight against the king or queen. Conversely, they may be used to drive away the bishop. The h-pawn may have an additional or alternative aim: to provide a bolt hole for the king in case a hostile queen or rook invades the first rank. Sometimes too these passive-looking moves may conceal a hidden threat: preparation for the advance of the b- or g-pawn.

From all of which you can see that pawns are extremely useful men. But they do have a weakness; they cannot retreat. That means that you have to be extra careful about advancing them. A charge with your pawns line abreast may be exhilarating and even intimidating, but it is unlikely to be sound.

BLACK

42

BLACK

43

Since pieces must give way to pawns as well as being blocked by them, the pawn structure, or skeleton as it is sometimes called, dominates the early stages of a game.

Let us forget the pieces for a moment and just look at a few pawn skeletons.

You will have little difficulty in identifying (42) as bad for Black, nor the reason for it: failure to contest the centre and a cramped position – the bishops have no choice of squares. Space confers flexibility and we shall consider this concept more fully later.

White's pawn structure in (42) is excellent. To establish safely pawns on d4 and e4 (or d5 and e5 in the case of Black) is an ideal that is often hard to achieve.

By contrast, (43) is good for both sides. White has occupied the centre and Black has contested it. White can advance his e-pawn further when Black will probably strike at its support with c5 and the position is about equal.

Notice that, if White allows it, Black would be able later to convert his weak pawn formation in (42) to the

122

much more favourable formation in (*43*). But that would mean moving the d-pawn a second time to attain a square that could have been reached in one move, which would be a loss of time. Time is another important opening idea which we shall look at often. Loss of time is usually more serious for Black than for White because he is already handicapped by having to move second.

Now, how would you evaluate the pawn position in (*44*)?

There is not much in it. Black has occupied the best central squares but White's moves also strike at the centre which, because the pawn pairs attack each other, is unstable.

We have seen that moving the f-pawn early in the game exposes the white king to slight risks (*7*). There can be danger of a queen check at h4 before castling and of a bishop check at c5 after castling – indeed a bishop at c5 can sometimes prevent castling. But here White has a purpose: to exchange the f-pawn for the opponent's e-pawn, thereby opening the f-file. When White castles (0–0), the rook on f1 will be bearing down on the enemy position. So there is yet another use for the pawn – to unblock files so that rooks can operate more effectively.

There are of course many other possible pawn skeletons, which may be mobile, where one or more pawns are able to advance, or static, where the pawns are locked together. However the pawns are structured, they will strongly influence, if not dictate, the development of the pieces and the subsequent play. Make no bones about it – pawn skeletons are important!

109 *The Time Factor*

Suppose White opens 1. c4 (*4*). Black could well respond with 1... e5. Does this position (*45*) strike you as familiar? Look back at (*14*) and you will see that it is identical – except for one thing; the colours are reversed.

So what is happening? Simply this: White is playing Black's defence but with the important difference that he has a move in hand.

There is no doubt that in chess, squares of alternating colour assist our perception of the board. As one early writer put it, 'The distinction of bicolored chequers is an elegant guide to the eye in diagonal movements.'

But the contrast can dazzle and sometimes blind. Did you notice at once the relationship between (*45*) and (*14*)?

It is helpful to look at openings, including those in this book, from both sides of the board. It is surprising how different the same position can appear and, more fruitfully, how the comparison can generate new ideas. (It is not uncommon for a master, when it is not his turn to play, to get up and look at the game from his opponent's angle.)

Another visual exercise that can be rewarding, though for less obvious reasons, is to view the board as black

with a pattern of white squares superimposed, and then reverse the image. This can also lead to revelations. It is a fact that chequered squares, as well as assisting the unpractised eye, can also beguile it into blunders by inflicting a temporary 'colour blindness'.

But back to the question of time which, as we have seen, when applied to the chessboard means moves, and not the time taken to make them.

One way to gain time is by giving up a pawn, or perhaps two, and rarely even a piece, to speed development. Such a sacrifice, commonly called a gambit, should not be undertaken lightly. Pawns, as we know, are like krugerrands, to be surrendered only for adequate compensation. If the defender is able to repel the subsequent attack and hold on to his extra material (a quaint term in vulgar use, meaning more or stronger men) then he should win. In theory, anyway.

This seems a good opportunity to examine a bona fide opening, at least for the first few moves, in which White goes for development at all costs.

	WHITE	BLACK
1.	e4	e5
2.	d4	exd4

The best move. Let us pause briefly to look at alternatives. Black might have tried to maintain a pawn on e5 by replying 2... d6; when after 3. dxe5 dxe5 White could stop Black castling by exchanging queens.

If Black had played 2 . . . f6 with the same idea, he would have been justly punished. White would have continued 3. dxe5, fxe5 (better for Black not to recapture); 4. Qh5+. This early sortie with the queen is condoned for the reason given previously; there are defects in the opponent's position that can be immediately exploited. As we remarked earlier, the move f3/f6 is almost invariably bad.

Now what is Black to do? If he blocks the queen with 4 . . . g6, White continues 5. Qxe5+ attacking both the king and the unguarded rook (*46*).

On the other hand, if he moves the king to avoid the loss of the rook, the sequel is rather worse: 4 . . . Ke7; 5. Qxe5+, Kf7; 6. Bc4+, d5 (if the king moves to g6, White gives checkmate with the queen); 7. Bxd5+ and Black will still be mated in a few moves unless he gives up his queen (*47*). A dreadful warning!

Another possibility might have been 2 . . . Nc6, when 3. d5 would have forced the knight to move again.

Now return to the main line.

3.	c3	

Instead of recapturing with the queen, when Black would gain time by attacking it with 3 . . . Nc6, White offers another pawn.

3.	...	dxc3

46

47

Black can here safely decline the gambit by, for example, striking in the centre with 3 . . . d5.

4.   Bc4

Yet another pawn on offer . . .

4.   ...   **cxb2**
5.   **Bxb2** (*48*)

Which side would you like to play? White has two
finely posted bishops and is well ahead in development,
but Black is two pawns to the good with no obvious
weaknesses. However, he will have to play carefully or
White's cavalier attack will bring home the bacon (the
opening is called the Danish Gambit, by the way).

BLACK

WHITE

48

Now turn the board round and look at the game from
Black's side.

Black has a splendid move here which you probably
would not have considered.

5.   ...   **d5!** (*49*)

is a cautious 'yes', but with an important distinction. White was committed there to castling on the king's side whereas here he would be foolish even to consider castling on the queen's side. Why not? Because the position is too open and two pawns, valuable as shields for a castled king, have departed.

BLACK

WHITE

74

A weakness is only a weakness if the other side can take advantage of it. Weaknesses can be temporary or permanent. Because pawns cannot retreat, and as often as not cannot advance without loss, pawn weaknesses are more likely to be permanent than piece weaknesses – that is, pieces posted on bad squares. Once a pawn has surrendered guard on a square it can never regain it.

So although the variations we have just been looking at were tactical, their origins were positional. From this we can draw a useful conclusion: positional weaknesses create tactical opportunities. From here we can proceed to the idea of provoking positional weaknesses as a viable strategy.

Try to force or entice disabling pawn advances and get the opponent's pieces onto bad squares – the tactical combinations that win material, or perhaps lead to mate, will then present themselves. Masters play positional chess as a matter of course – they would never achieve mastery unless they did. In your games, you are in the habit, from time to time, of overlooking lethal checks and undefended men, and probably hope that your opponent will do likewise which is why you are inclined to play on long after you should have given up. Strong players rarely overlook such things. When they crack, it is usually because their position has become untenable, like Black's in the opening we have been looking at.

119

While you are thinking about that, follow through the next opening which is something a little more orthodox. Again a Queen's Gambit, but this time Black declines the pawn and instead fortifies the centre.

	WHITE	BLACK
1.	d4	d5
2.	c4	e6

If Black had defended with 2. . . Nf6, White would have captured in the centre and then brought out the queen's knight or advanced the king's pawn, depending on whether Black recaptured with the queen or knight respectively, so gaining time.

	WHITE	BLACK
3.	Nc3	Nf6
4.	Bg5	Nbd7

Doesn't that lose a pawn?

5.	cxd5	exd5
6.	Nxd5	Nxd5!
7.	Bxd8	Bb4+
8.	Qd2	Bxd2+
9.	Kxd2	Kxd8 (75)

White has lost a piece for a pawn. Black could have played instead 8... Kxd8 since the white queen cannot escape. Sometimes it is wise to defer a capture under these circumstances.

Do not seek any profound meaning in this little trap, but it serves to remind you that there can be pitfalls in the most innocent-looking positions. Never play 'obvious' moves without taking a second look.

BLACK

WHITE

75

120

A more natural move for Black, since it prepares to castle and does not block a piece, is 4 . . . Be7. Let's start again.

	WHITE	BLACK
1.	d4	d5
2.	c4	e6
3.	Nc3	Nf6
4.	Bg5	Be7

Exemplary play by both sides. White is putting pressure on Black's centre and is in no hurry to develop his king's side pieces since his king is not in danger. Black has a small problem – how to develop his queen's bishop effectively. A feature of the gambit accepted is that this bishop can be developed before moving the e-pawn, a benefit offset by ceding temporary advantage in the centre to White – the 'give and take' syndrome. Another idea: Black can defer the capture of the gambit pawn until after White has developed his king's bishop, forcing it to move again. White on the other hand will not be keen to anticipate this by playing cxd5 since this would allow Black to recapture with his e-pawn, so freeing the bishop.

Black plans to free his bishop by advancing the e-pawn at the right moment. He cannot do this while his d-pawn is under threat. You should now be able to follow the logic behind the next few moves.

	WHITE	BLACK
5.	Nf3	0–0
6.	e3	Nbd7
7.	Rc1	c6
8.	Bd3	dxc4
9.	Bxc4	Nd5
10.	Bxe7	Qxe7
11.	0–0	Nxc3
12.	Rxc3	e5 (76)

Black has achieved his objective though White still has a faint edge. You should experiment with other ideas for Black; for example, by playing b6 and bringing

the bishop into play via b7 – this placing of the bishop is known as the fianchetto. Also, did you wonder at the purpose of the passive 7 . . . c6? Without that white rook looking down the file you could have considered c5.

Whatever you do as Black, you must not allow your queen's bishop to be shut in (White has no such problems). A piece out of play is a piece minus. Even if you are ahead in material, do not be tempted into complacency. Untold games have been won by the side with the weaker forces. It is usually the case that the winner has been able to concentrate his forces in the right place at the right time. What's the good of being a rook and a bishop ahead if both are on their original squares when your king gets mated in the middle of the board?

121 *An Orthodox Opening*

The next opening, known as the Four Knights for obvious reasons, can be described as orthodox because it follows closely an opening axiom that has been around a long time: knights out first, then bishops. Like a lot of good advice it is hardly profound since this is the natural order of things anyway – the knights develop freely and the mandatory pawn advance in the centre will release at least one bishop. It is an axiom to honour in the spirit but, as we have seen, not always in the letter.

	WHITE	BLACK
1.	e4	e5
2.	Nf3	Nc6
3.	Nc3	Nf6
4.	Bb5	Bb4
5.	0–0	0–0
6.	d3	d6 (77)

BLACK

WHITE

77

Symmetrical play and model development. Does this suggest to you that a good strategy for Black might be to imitate White's moves? Forget it. It may indeed be wise on occasion to copy your opponent's play for a few moves but only if your moves can be justified in their own right. In any case, the strategy will fail sooner or later if only because the first player gives check. An example, 1. e4, e5; 2. d4, d5; 3. dxe5, dxe4; 4. Qxd8+. How is Black going to mimic that? Or again, 1. e4, e5; 2. d4, d5; 3. exd5, exd4; 3. Qxd4 and Black is hardly likely to be tempted by 4. . . . Qxd5.

Let us continue . . .

7.	Bg5	Bg4
8.	Nd5	

Now White threatens to capture soon on f6 with one of his pieces, forcing Black to recapture with the pawn, thereby gravely weakening the black squares around the king and exposing him to attack up the file. Black must perforce continue to ape White's play.

8.	...	Nd4
9.	Nxb4	Nxb5
10.	Nd5	Nd4
11.	Qd2 (78)	

BLACK

WHITE

78

Dare Black continue 11 ... Qd7? He dare not. 11 ...
Qd7; 12. Bxf6, Bxf3; 13. Ne7+ (now the dance must
stop), Kh8; 14. Bxg7+, Kxg7; 15. Qg5+, Kh8; 16. Qf6
mate. A bit drastic, but it proves the point. Don't take
this as any sort of norm – ten successive imitative moves
is rare indeed.

None of the rooks took any part in the play. This is
not at all unusual in a short game. Tucked away in the
wings when the curtain goes up, the rooks are usually
the last actors to come on stage.

122

Another example of play in the Four Knights' game:

	WHITE	BLACK
1.	e4	e5
2.	Nf3	Nc6
3.	Nc3	Nf6
4.	Bb5	Bb4
5.	0–0	0–0
6.	d3	Bxc3

So far a model of rapid development. Black
exchanged bishop for knight here because the knight
was likely to prove a better piece than the bishop. For
example, White might later have played Bg5 followed by
Nd5 when the black bishop's only use would have been
in defence.

	WHITE	BLACK
7.	bxc3	d6
8.	Bg5	Qe7

Black's last move is not easy to understand. It does
three things: it prepares to unite the rooks after a bishop
move, it gives additional protection to the e-pawn which
may be needed if White plays d4 (Black would not wish

to exchange this pawn as this would undouble the white pawns and also give ground in the centre) and lastly it prepares Black's next move which is part of his plan. Check from the diagram that you have the position right.

79

Position after Black's
8th move

80

Position after White's
13th move

9.	Re1	Nd8
10.	d4	Ne6

Another way to attack a pinning bishop.

11. Bc1

Sometimes a bishop returns home and then comes out on the other diagonal. White has the better of the opening with more space in the centre and some attacking chances. Black's e-pawn is weak and to exchange it for White's d-pawn would only strengthen the white centre. If Black now developed the bishop with 11... Bd7; and White played 12. Bc4 (if 12. Bxd7, Nxd7!), then 12... Bc6? (with the idea of meeting 13. dxe5 with Nxe4) would be a terrible mistake on account of 13. d5!

(remember the pawn fork (40*D*)? This might-have-happened disaster earns a diagram (page 169, right).

123   *The Quiet Game*

The favourite opening to initiate beginners is the Giuoco Piano, the 'Quiet Game', one of the first openings ever recorded. Its potentialities are near to exhaustion – at least, that is the present view – so it does not appear often in master practice. However, the opening is popular amongst less-exalted chessplayers and rightly so, since, apart from being sound, it adheres closely to all the principles of good opening play. It is not always as quiet as its name suggests – you can get some quite wild games with the Giuoco Piano.

	WHITE	BLACK
1.	e4	e5
2.	Nf3	Nc6
3.	Bc4	Bc5
4.	c3 (*81*)	

This is a lively continuation.

The text takes away the best square for the queen's knight but the deprivation is temporary. White's aggressive intentions are obvious, Black's defence less so. The dozy 4. d3 would allow Black to develop undisturbed.

4.	...	Nf6

It is a good general rule that when you are perplexed for a move, perhaps because the impending complications extend out of sight, opt for the natural one – as here, it is probably best.

5.	d4	exd4
6.	cxd4	

You can see that to take with the knight would be out of harmony with the idea behind White's fourth move. Also, White has no intention of donating his e-pawn without a proper return.

6.	...	Bb4+
7.	Nc3	Nxe4
8.	0–0	Bxc3
9.	d5 (*82*)	

White is a piece and a pawn behind – but not for long. The text keeps the attack going and has the virtue of denying Black the freeing d5. Not everyone's idea of a quiet game.

| 9. | ... | Bf6 |
| 10. | Re1 | |

Keeping up the pressure. Black still has two pieces attacked.

171

10.	...	Ne7

Black must be very careful for his king is still in the centre. An easy mistake here would be 10... Ne5; 11. Nxe5, Bxe5; 12. Rxe4 with 13. f4 after Black defends the bishop.

11.	Rxe4	d6 (*83*)

BLACK   WHITE

WHITE   BLACK

82   83

Let us assess the position. Black has scrambled a defence and is now prepared to castle. White has more space, a strong centre (although his king's bishop is temporarily blocked) and is well ahead in development – but he is a pawn short, which leaves the chances approximately even.

The problem for White is to find a weak point which his superior mobility will allow him to exploit. Time is at a premium. Black's pawn skeleton is uncompromised and his minor pieces will soon find good squares, and if that happens the extra pawn should begin to make its presence felt.

It is normal for a knight to be posted at f3/f6 rather than a bishop. There a knight defends the h-pawn, often the weak point in a castled position. (The weak point in the position of an uncastled king is f2/f7, the focus of many opening attacks.)

So White here has a target of sorts – the h-pawn. This leads sensibly to White's next move.

| 12. | Bg5 | Bxg5 |
| 13. | Nxg5 | |

Black has been forced to exchange off his only developed piece. The alternative of 12... 0–0; 13. Bxf6, gxf6, could not be seriously contemplated on account of the shattered pawn defences. The position is about level.

124

Here is another example of play in the Giuoco Piano:

	WHITE	BLACK
1.	e4	e5
2.	Nf3	Nc6
3.	Bc4	Bc5

'Knights out first, and then bishops' is an old saying and good advice.

4.	c3

Preparing the advance of the d-pawn. White strives for a strong pawn centre.

4.	...	Nf6

Black counters by attacking the undefended e-pawn.

| 5. | d4 | exd4 |
| 6. | cxd4 | Bb4+ |

Black had no time to take the e-pawn because his bishop was attacked.

7. Bd2

Black could now play 7... Nxe4; and there might follow 8. Bxb4, Nxb4; 9. Bxf7+ (a temporary sacrifice that regains the pawn), Kxf7; 10. Qb3+, followed by Qxb4 and an equal game.

| 7. | ... | Bxd2+ |

| 84 | 85 |
| Position after White's 7th move | Position after Black's 11th move |

8. Nbxd2

Now White guards the e-pawn whilst developing a piece.

| 8. | ... | d5 |

It was essential for Black to counter White's strong centre. White will now be left with an isolated d-pawn, a situation common to several openings (in the game in Part Five, White got an isolated d-pawn in quite a different way). The positional weakness of this pawn is balanced by its influence on the centre.

| 9. | exd5 | Nxd5 |
| 10. | Qb3 | Nce7 |

Defending the king's knight which is twice attacked. Black could not move the threatened piece because he would lose a pawn (to 11. Bxf7+) when also his king would be unable to castle. A king who cannot castle in the opening is in a dangerous position. Notice the white queen has come out to a square where she exerts pressure but cannot well be attacked.

| 11. | 0–0 | 0–0 |

Both sides move their king to safety (see diagram). White will now play his rooks to files where their powers can be better used – probably to the c- and e-files. Black has still to develop his bishop but has an about equal game, thanks to his strong knight on d5.

125   *An Outrageous Gambit*

An otherwise respectable sea captain, called Evans, is credited with the outrageous gambit which has borne his name for the last 150 years. The Evans is a bold alternative for White at the fourth move of the Giuoco Piano.

	WHITE	BLACK
1.	e4	e5
2.	Nf3	Nc6
3.	Bc4	Bc5
4.	b4 (*86*)	

This intemperate advance turns out to be not only playable but positively dangerous, requiring careful play by Black. To decline the pawn is to give White a considerable advantage in space.

It is a general, though by no means universal, principle that the best way to defuse a gambit is to accept it and then to return the material at a propitious moment.

BLACK   BLACK

WHITE
86   WHITE
87

4.   ...   **Bxb4**

If 4... Nxb4 White continues as in the main variation, with advantage. He must not be tempted by 5. Nxe5?, Qf6!; and now White cannot reply 6. d4 on account of 6 ... Bxd4; 7. Qxd4, Nxc2+; followed by Nxd4 – that fork again! No better is 5. Nxe5?, Qf6!; 6. Bxf7+, Kf8; and Black has too many threats.

5.   c3   **Ba5**
6.   d4 (*87*)

176

The play hereon can get highly involved. White has sacrificed for rapid development and must turn this to advantage whereas Black will be anxious to get his king to safety as quickly as possible. In similar positions White can sometimes delay or even arrest Black castling by Ba3.

Always be on the look out for ideas like this and see if they can be made to work, it is not a bad way to tackle the openings. Contemplate ideal squares for your men then plan to get them there. If you can't, look round for a second-best plan.

For example, in (87) Black might reasonably decide that his priority is to castle. To do this he must bring the knight out. Is 6 . . . Nf6 playable? No, because after 7. dxe5, Nxe4; 8. Qd5 the stray knight is forfeit on account of the threat 9. Qxf7 mate. So the weakness on e5 must first be attended to. There appear to be two reasonable alternatives: 6 . . . exd4, removing the aggressor and also stopping White's queen reaching d5; and 6 . . . d6, which anchors the e-pawn. In fact, both these moves are playable.

It is a popular myth that chess masters examine in depth all the possible moves for both sides at each turn of play. Most possibilities the expert dismisses at a glance on the strength of his experience (which you are just starting to accumulate) or instinct (which is subconscious experience). Only when he has welded his ideas into a plan does he actually look at move sequences. You should try to do this too. Always have a plan. A bad plan is better than no plan at all, as every chess writer has counselled since the introduction of movable type. Beware the King-Kong approach of 'Time-I-moved-the bishop-where-shall-I-move-it-to?'

126 *A Tempting Target*

One plan that might occur to you is to attack f7, the weak point in the enemy defences, with minor pieces.

(You scorn the idea of an immediate attack on it with the queen – a beginner's folly.)

	WHITE	BLACK
1.	e4	e5
2.	Nf3	Nc6
3.	Bc4	Nf6
4.	Ng5	

This move offends our opening precepts but f7 is a tempting target.

A threat can be met in one of two ways, and sometimes both simultaneously: it can be resisted or it can be ignored in favour of a counter attack. Surprisingly, Black has an adequate counter here in 4 . . . Bc5, striking at White's weak point. (If you want to know more, you will have to look up a heavy book on the openings!) But let's see what happens if Black resists.

	WHITE	BLACK
4.	...	d5
5.	exd5	Nxd5

Black does better to attack the bishop with 5 . . . Na5 and complicated play to follow. Now White is faced with a further and bigger temptation.

	WHITE	BLACK
6.	Nxf7	Kxf7
7.	Qf3+	Ke6

The knight is twice attacked and must be defended.

	WHITE	BLACK
8.	Nc3	Nb4
9.	Qe4 (88)	

White guards against the knight fork of king and rook and prepares to drive the piece back with 10. a3. Moreover, White threatens d4 and then, if necessary, f4

or Bf4 when Black's pinned e-pawn will fall. Now Black has only 9 . . . c6 to save his piece and he must abide the coming storm. In practice, White is likely to win.

Something more must be said about White's fourth move. Apart from deflecting a piece from the centre and failing to implement development, this knight adventure fractures another opening maxim: 'Do not move any piece twice until you've moved every piece once.' In few openings can this advice be followed literally, but the principle is a good one just the same.

In this case the move works because there is a clear reason behind it. To delay the attack would be to forgo it. We remarked earlier that it is sometimes wise to postpone a move, but the reverse is more often true. Be awake to opportunity; if your opponent lifts his guard you are likely to have only that one chance to take advantage of it. Developing your pieces is fine, but routine development is myopic. Remember to think through every move.

But to return to that knight move. As a general rule, the move Nb5/g5, or Nb4/g4 by Black, is a deplorable begin-ners' habit. Sometimes quite vacuous, sometimes aimed at a fork on c7/f7, or c2/f2 by Black, if the opponent obliges, the move is usually no more than a time-wasting gesture. The sortie can be justified only if it constitutes a threat. If the threat is easily countered, then a valid excuse for the move might be to advance the c/f-pawn with the intention of withdrawing the knight behind it.

127 *Storm in the Centre*

Another idea for White in this opening is to strike at once in the centre. This can lead to the Max Lange attack where things like positional play and pawn skeletons are temporarily abandoned in a lively punch-up.

	WHITE	BLACK
1.	e4	e5
2.	Nf3	Nc6
3.	Bc4	Nf6
4.	d4	exd4
5.	0–0	Bc5
6.	e5 (*89*)	

BLACK   WHITE

WHITE   BLACK

89   90

| 6. | ... | d5 |

The counter attack. Now things get a bit hairy.

7.	exf6	dxc4
8.	Re1+	Be6
9.	Ng5 (*90*)	

Another example of a justified knight advance. White can safely delay fxg7 – can't he?

| 9. | ... | Qd5 |

I hope you considered, and rejected, 9 . . . Qxf6?; 10. Nxe6, fxe6; 11. Qh5+ – see the undefended bishop?

10. Nc3!

The knight cannot be taken because the pinned bishop does not defend the queen.

| 10. | ... | Qf5 |

WHITE

BLACK

91

11. Nce4　　　　　**0–0–0** (*91*)

A case where queen's side castling is called for. To castle on the king's side in face of White's wicked pawn would be suicidal. The pawn could still not be safely taken: 11... gxf6?; 12. g4. Now the queen is overloaded and Black must lose a piece – or worse. Work out the alternatives.

128　　　　　　　　　*Order Please!*

The key position in the Max Lange (*89*) can be reached by playing the opening moves in any of several different orders. The sequence in which moves are made is nearly always important. Where this is not the case, you may still, by playing move A before B, either permit or deny options to your opponent.

It can happen that identical positions can be reached from quite different openings, perhaps with colours reversed, and not just different sequences of moves within the same opening. This is known in chess jargon as transposition. If you are playing the opening intelligently, as I trust you now are, a transposition should be of passing academic interest, but recognition that one has occurred may help you to focus onto the possibilities. To take a simple case, supposing you began 1. f4 (Bird's Opening, named after its practitioner, not because it's on the wing). Your opponent could reply with 1 . . . e5. This is an ingenious gambit. If you take the pawn at once (2. fxe5), Black continues with 2 . . . d6; when after 3. exd6, Bxd6, Black is threatening mate in three starting with a queen check and gets a good game for the pawn sacrificed. Perhaps that prospect does not appeal to you? Never mind: you have the possibility of transposing into the King's Gambit with 2. e4, which may not appeal to Black who perhaps for this reason deliberately avoids replying to 1. e4 with

1 . . . e5. This leads us on to consider psychology as a weapon in the chess openings.

129
Know Your Enemy

In your choice of an opening or defence there are a number of extraneous factors to think about not least of which is your opponent, a rather complex organism who may at the same time be thinking about you.

Psychology can play a significant role in a chess game, and particularly in the opening. Masters sometimes ponder their first few moves (which are second nature to them) on this account.

On one occasion, a tournament game opened 1. e4, e6; 2. Bb5. The rationale behind White's extraordinary second move was that Black, a rigid theoretician, invariably responded 2 . . . d5 in this opening and could not now do so. More, if the bishop were driven away so that Black could proceed with his plan, it would inevitably move to a better square. The master who was playing Black was therefore faced with a dilemma. He spent 15 minutes over his reply and eventually lost.

This is not an example to emulate, merely an extreme case of psychology that paid off. If you have heeded the advice in this book and are prepared to experiment with all openings you will be to some extent immune from shock tactics. If your opponent is a chess computer, then the risk of it exploiting your psychological weaknesses is minimal, though I wouldn't bank on that state of affairs lasting for ever. At this stage in your chess career it would be wiser to forget your opponent altogether and play the position before you. You are concerned with gaining experience, not with winning games – that will come later.

130
A Pawn Charge

A chess game is an indivisible conflict. For convenience, one talks of the opening, the middle game and the end game, but in practice the divisions are blurred and largely meaningless. In planning your first moves you should consider their long- as well as their short-term consequences. Pawn advances in particular require that you take a distant perspective.

The idea behind many opening variations is to establish an end-game advantage, and that is most certain to include a superior pawn skeleton. A passed pawn – one that cannot be stopped in its march to promotion by an opposing pawn – is always strong provided it can be supported, for it needs a piece to check its progress, a distasteful duty for the defence.

Advanced pawns can be game winners – or losers. In the ending, when the queens have left the board and risk of checkmate is negligible, the kings become powerful pieces. Forward pawns whose support is weak or cut can be destroyed by an invading king when your king is likely to be far from the scene. It is important to consider the after-effects of what appears to be a promising advance.

Let us get one thing clear – and it deserves capitals – PASSIVE DEFENCE INVARIABLY FAILS. This applies to all openings and nowhere is it better illustrated than when facing a pawn charge. At times of course you are obliged to ward off threats with wretched little moves that create pawn weaknesses or involve humiliating retreats. But if you fix firmly the idea that a menacing pawn can, with vigorous counterplay, be turned into a distressed stray, then you are going to be looking for the right sort of moves.

	WHITE	BLACK
1.	d4	Nf6
2.	c4	g6
3.	Nc3	Bg7
4.	e4	d6
5.	f4 (92)	

Frightening, isn't it? Keep cool. Here you might consider 5... c5, hitting at once at White's active centre but let's suppose that you decide to remove your king from the path of the avalanche. This formation for Black is quite common against openings which begin with 1. d4. It offers security and prepares to contest the centre with either e5 or c5. To omit both would invite suffocation.

5.	...	0–0
6.	Nf3	c6
7.	Be2	Nfd7
8.	Be3	e5
9.	fxe5	dxe5
10.	d5	f5
11.	Qb3	Na6
12.	0–0–0 *(93)*	

BLACK   WHITE

WHITE   BLACK

93   94

131

Black's counter in the centre was tardy. Now White has the certain prospect of a dangerous passed pawn on the d-file.

On the other hand, an early advance by White, pushing Black back, could prove premature for the cramp may only be temporary. Continue from (*92*).

5.	...	0–0
6.	e5	Ne8
7.	Be3	c5

This pawn sacrifice crumbles White's centre and is justified because White is behind in development – all his king's side pieces are still indoors.

8.	dxc5

Black cannot recapture because his queen is unguarded – so he develops another piece.

8.	...	Nc6
9.	cxd6	exd6 (*94*)

Play might continue 10. Nf3, Qa5; 11. exd6, Nxd6; 12. Qxd6, Bxc3+; 13. bxc3, Qxc3+ followed by Qxa1. This fork of king and rook is a recurring theme in the openings. Observe that after 10. Nf3, dxe5? would not be a good idea. 11. Qxd8, Nxd8; and White has 12. Bc5, winning rook for bishop, yet another common theme in the openings. On the field of strategy, the ground is thick with tactics.

132

It is a widely held belief that the first several moves of a chess game are dull. After all, each side is just concerned with getting its pieces out; the fun starts later. The idea of pawn promotion, for example, seems absurd. How can a humble foot soldier advancing but one step at a time hope, in the early stages of a game, to break through the massed ranks of the enemy and achieve glory? To show you what can happen, given a lot of imagination and a little luck, here are two enthronements, the same theme in different openings and on opposite sides of the board.

	WHITE	BLACK
1.	d4	d5
2.	Nf3	Bf5
3.	c4	c6
4.	Qb3	Qb6
5.	cxd5	Qxb3
6.	axb3	Bxb1
7.	dxc6	Be4
8.	Rxa7!	Rxa7
9.	c7 and queens (*95*)	

BLACK WHITE

WHITE

95

BLACK

96

	WHITE	BLACK
1.	e4	c6
2.	d4	d5
3.	Nc3	dxe4
4.	Nxe4	Nf6
5.	Ng3	h5
6.	Bg5	h4
7.	Bxf6	hxg3
8.	Be5	Rxh2
9.	Rxh2	Qa5+!
10.	c3	Qxe5+!
11.	dxe5	gxh2 (*96*)

And Black ends up a piece ahead.

133 *A Combative Defence*

The Sicilian Defence is characterised by 1... c5, in answer to 1. e4 (*14*). It is a popular Black reply to White's opening move. It creates an immediate imbalance in the centre and usually leads to a lively if not exciting game.

	WHITE	BLACK
1.	e4	c5
2.	Nf3	Nc6
3.	d4 (97)	

WHITE

BLACK

97

Not good would have been 2. d4, cxd4; 3. Qxd4, Nc6; when the queen must move again – but you knew that, didn't you? White could have instead prepared d4 with 2. c3 but that would have allowed Black to continue 2 . . . d5; and after 3. exd5, Qxd5; White is deprived of the time-gaining Nc3.

To establish pawns securely side-by-side on e4 and d4 is an ideal. Heed the word 'securely'. In some openings one side – usually White on account of having the first move – is able to occupy these squares briefly, but is unable to maintain his pawns there.

Pawns at e4/d4 (e5/d5) are strong because they command a line of four vital squares in the enemy position. If one of these pawns is forced to advance, then not only is the number of squares attacked reduced to three, but these are all of one colour, ceding pawn control in the centre of the squares of the opposite colour. This is not to suggest that you must not advance a pawn in the centre beyond the fourth rank. The mobility conferred by pawns on e4/d4 (e5/d5) permits an advance at a time of the player's choosing.

Black's second move above is natural, but he has the choice of good alternatives: for instance, 2 . . . d6; 2 . . . e6; and 2 . . . g6. Each of these leads to distinctive systems, markedly different one from the other. The Sicilian Defence is rich in strategies which accounts in part for its enduring favour.

3.	...	cxd4
4.	Nxd4	Nf6
5.	Nc3	d6
6.	Bg5	e6
7.	Qd2	Be7
8.	0–0–0	0–0 (*98*)

WHITE

BLACK

98

134

Black almost invariably castles on the king's side in the Sicilian but White, depending on the system adopted, may castle on either side. Where he castles on the queen's side, as here, the way is open for both sides to attack the enemy king without restraint.

It is unlikely that an attack with pieces alone can succeed. At least one pawn must be enlisted for the assault. The a/h-pawn is a favourite for this task since when it is exchanged for the opposing b/g-pawn – the usual aim – the rook behind it will come alive with an open file on which to operate.

When the kings face each other on the same side of the board, an attacker who plans a pawn assault must agonize about the consequent weakening of his own king's position. No such problems exist in (98). White will charge with the h-pawn but Black has already an open line on which to operate – the c-file. A sacrifice which sometimes succeeds here is for Black to give up his queen's rook for White's queen's knight to gain advantage in the centre and to disturb the White king position. It is usually a matter of who gets there first, and that means that in situations like this it is unwise to waste time on defensive moves that are likely to be no more than palliatives anyway. Bust or be busted!

A well-tried line in the Sicilian pivots on the capture by Black of a remote pawn. The practice of pawn-grabbing has its advocates and detractors and nowhere more so than in this variation, known as the Poisoned Pawn.

	WHITE	BLACK
1.	e4	c5
2.	Nf3	d6
3.	d4	cxd4
4.	Nxd4	Nf6

5.	Nc3	a6
6.	Bg5	e6
7.	f4	Qb6
8.	Qd2	Qxb2 (*99*)

The theory of this sacrifice is akin to that of most gambits – to displace an enemy man and to hasten development. Here the queen is out of play for at least two moves and White gets an open file for his queen's rook. On the other hand, if Black can hold onto the pawn and develop safely, then the extra man should serve him well later. An example of play, which we discussed earlier, where opening strategy is directed towards the end game.

WHITE BLACK

BLACK WHITE

99 100

Play might continue:

9.	Rb1	Qa3
10.	e5	dxe5
11.	fxe5	Nfd7

12.	Bc4	Bb4
13.	Rb3	Qa5
14.	0–0	0–0 (*100*)

Black runs for cover while he has time. Latest analysis suggests that the Poisoned Pawn variation is ... but there, we can safely leave theory to the scholars and screwballs – it will be different tomorrow anyway.

135

| | WHITE | BLACK |
| 1. | e4 | c5 |

This is currently one of the most popular defences to the king's pawn opening (chess openings go in and out of fashion like other things). Black's move unbalances the central pawn position and is the signal for a hard fight.

2.	Nf3	d6
3.	d4	cxd4
4.	Nxd4	Nf6
5.	Nc3	a6

This move was played to prevent the square b5 being used by one of the white minor pieces, and to prepare an advance of the b-pawn which would allow the QB to be developed at b7. We saw this same idea in the game in **91**. Black also plans an attack on the queen's side, so this move combines both attack and defence.

| 6. | Bg5 | e6 |

Black permits the pin. For one reason, he must get his King's bishop out.

7.	f4	Be7
8.	Qf3	Qc7 (*101*)

This move stops both the advance of the e-pawn and the development of white's bishop at the good square c4. Check your position against the diagram.

9.   0–0–0

101   102

Another case of queen's-side castling. The rook is at once activated and White will now be free to advance the king's-side pawns to attack the black king's position. Black will probably have to castle on the king's side as he has weakened the pawn position on the queen's side.

9.	...	Nbd7
10.	Bd3	b5 (*102*)

The position offers many tactical possibilities and the chances are about even. White now has the double attack 11. e5, threatening the knight and at the same time uncovering a queen attack on the rook. However, Black too has tactical play and all sorts of violence could follow. This is a typical Sicilian scrap, wild and complicated.

As a general guide, free pawns in the centre are always worth grabbing whilst gift pawns in the aisles should be judged on the merits of the position.

By contrast to the Sicilian, the mirror defence 1. d4, f5, known as the Dutch, is rarely played. The reason we have already met: Black's pawn advance loosens slightly his king's position. He will not be able to develop quickly enough to castle on the queen's side.

136   *Disarming the Bishop Guard*

A bishop entrenched at b2/g2 or b7/g7 is known as a fianchettoed bishop (fianchetto is a term derived from the Italian, meaning 'side moves'). It affords one of the strongest defensive positions for a castled king, particularly with the help of a knight at c3/f3 or c6/f6 respectively.

There are two common ways of attacking this defence structure. One way is by advancing the a/h-pawn and exchanging it for the b/g-pawn, creating an open rook's file. Here the rook, perhaps joined by the queen or a minor piece, can attack the defence's weak point at a2/h2 or a7/h7 respectively. The other way is to force the exchange of the entrenched bishop. This is achieved by an artificial-looking manoeuvre which is effective only if the attacker has sufficient forces in hand to press the advantage. We can see this action live in our next opening.

WHITE	BLACK
1. **d4**	**c5**

A safe gambit. If White captured 2. dxc5, Black could retake the pawn at once after 2 ... Qa5+ but would be unwise to do so since it would leave the queen exposed to attack. The pawn cannot be held, and Black will recapture at leisure. The opening is known as the Benoni.

2.	c4	Nf6
3.	d5	e6
4.	Nc3	exd5
5.	cxd5	d6 (*103*)

Black has now the pawn majority on the queen's side in return for a backward pawn. A queen's side majority is an advantage where both sides castle on the king's side because the pawns can be advanced without jeopardizing the king.

In theory, and usually in practice, the majority can eventually be converted into a passed pawn. Face three pawns against two in their starting positions, remove the rest of the men from the board, and prove to yourself that this is so.

Black's backward pawn on d6 however is a permanent weakness and will have to be guarded constantly. A backward pawn is weak because it cannot be defended by another pawn.

WHITE

BLACK

103

6.	Nf3	g6
7.	Nd2	Bg7
8.	Nc4	

White deploys the knight to a square where it attacks Black's weak pawn: an example of identifying a weakness and setting out methodically to exploit it. White has time to do this because the centre is static.

8.	...	0–0
9.	Bf4	Ne8

Black must defend the pawn. A sacrifice is out of the question because, with the pawn on d6 gone, White's d-pawn would be passed.

10. Qd2 (*104*)

Now White is in a position to force the exchange of black-squared bishops after 11. Bh6, and any attempt by Black to avert the exchange will work out badly.

WHITE   BLACK

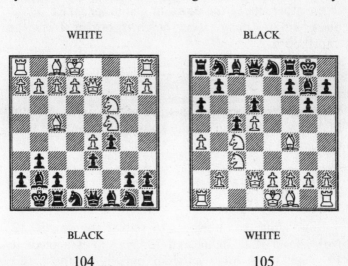

BLACK   WHITE

104   105

Black should never consider a move like Bxc3 except in extremity because this would seriously weaken the black squares round his king.

White may be in no hurry to force the exchange. It is sometimes a good idea to lodge a piece at h6 and then to advance the h-pawn. The defence may have trouble stopping the manoeuvre h4, h5, hxg6 when the rook joins in the attack. Without a piece at h6, the advance h4 is often best met by a like move.

Black needs to mobilise the queen's side quickly in order to counter White's threatened attack on the king's side and to capitalise on his pawn majority. He would like to drive away the well-placed knight on c4 but must first prepare the advance.

| 10. | ... | a6 |
| 11. | a4 (*105*) | |

Take in carefully White's reply. This is the usual way of stopping the advance of the b-pawn. (Later on, White might even bring his rook to a3 and then switch it to the other side of the board to join in the attack on the black king – imagination borrows heavily from the unorthodox.)

137

Suppose White omitted this preventive move and carried on with his plan on the king's side. Continue from (*104*).

| 10. | ... | a6 |
| 11. | Bh6 | b5 |

Now White has nowhere to retreat the knight. 12. Ne3 allows 12... Bxh6, and 12. Na3 loses a piece to 12... b4; (it is quite easy, in pursuit of the higher strategy, to overlook tactical trifles – take comfort that even world champions succumb on occasion). The text allows no option; White must take the bishop.

12.	**Bxg7**	**N (or K) xg7**
13.	**Ne3** (*106*)	

106

The position is transformed. Black's pawn majority is making ground, his backward pawn is out of danger and he has an open file for his major pieces. Also, he can switch his queen's rook quickly to the centre via a7.

By contrast, White's set-up is wretched and his prospects rather worse. The king's knight has still not completed his travels and the queen's knight can be chivvied at any time by b4. The advance 13... b4 at once is probably not Black's best even though the knight will have to retreat. If 14. Ne4?, f5; 15. Ng3, f4; and it's that pawn fork again! The drawback of Black's 13th move is that it will allow White's awkward knight back into c4: better to wait until it has moved away before teasing the queen's knight.

A solid defence system with clear positional aims is the French: 1. e4 e6 (*15*). Black allows White to build an impressive pawn centre and then seeks to undermine it to reach a favourable ending. Although the strategy is fairly straightforward, it is liable to be upset by tactical ploys; these facts-of-life that surface unexpectedly in all openings – look back at (*55*).

	WHITE	BLACK
1.	e4	e6
2.	d4	d5

The habitual first moves. Now White has significant options; he can exchange pawns, which avoids complications but gives him little advantage, he can bring out his queen's knight to guard the e-pawn, or he can push the e-pawn forward to give a classical French centre formation.

3.	e5	c5
4.	c3	Nc6
5.	Nf3	Qb6
6.	Be2 (*107*)	

White might be tempted into 6. Bd3 here in the hope that Black takes the offered pawn: 6 . . . cxd4; 7. cxd4 Nxd4? 8. Nxd4, Qxd4?; 9. Bb5+ and the black queen is feeling unwell (*108*). However, we have stressed that you should not be seduced by schemes that require your opponent to make a mistake. If after 6... cxd4; 7. cxd4, Black plays quietly 7 . . . Bd7 the threat on the pawn is real and White must either sacrifice or put pride to one side and move the bishop again. Return to (*107*).

6.	...	cxd4

7.	cxd4	Nge7

WHITE   WHITE

BLACK   BLACK

107   108

White's d-pawn is weak because it has been deprived of pawn support. Now Black is threatening to win it with 8... Nf5 and if White brings up a third defender (9. Be3) he loses the b-pawn to the queen.

8.	b3	Nf5
9.	Bb2	Bb4+
10.	Kf1	

Otherwise White loses the d-pawn.

10.	...	h5 (*109*)

To stop 11. g4 when the knight would have to go to h6 where it would be out of play. If the knight were withdrawn to e7, this would cut off the bishop retreat – these two pieces are inclined to interfere with each other in the French. After 10 . . . Bd7; 11. g4, Nfe7; 12. a3, Ba5; 13. b4 Black loses a piece for two pawns, a poor bargain. (Notice

201

though that White will first have to do something about his undefended bishop. Fortunately, the quarry cannot escape.) White may be planning to move his g-pawn anyway, to allow the king to move up and release the rook. The text (10… h5) discourages this plan. Although White has forfeited the right to castle, he has blunted the attack and now Black's pieces stand awkwardly.

WHITE

BLACK

109

139

A popular line in the French is shaped by an early pin:

	WHITE	BLACK
1.	e4	e6
2.	d4	d5
3.	Nc3	Bb4

Now White's e-pawn is undefended.

A knight at c3, pinned by a bishop against king or queen, is one of the commonest stratagems in the openings. When executing a pin, you should anticipate an immediate attack on your piece and be clear on the action you intend. To withdraw a bishop along the diagonal on which it arrived is to lose time; avoid it unless your opponent, in driving you away, has somehow weakened his position. The choice is then between capturing the pinned piece or retreating the bishop whilst maintaining the pin. The latter is often a good plan since although the initial a3 is unlikely to weaken the defender's position significantly and may indeed improve it, the follow-up b4, releasing the pin by shutting out the bishop, may not be wise, especially if the player's king is castled, or intends to seek sanctuary, on that side of the board.

4.	e5	c5
5.	a3 (*110*)	

WHITE   WHITE

BLACK   BLACK

110   111

Now Black, has three good options: he can withdraw, maintaining the pin, exchange the minor pieces or capture on d5 attacking the pinned knight.

5.	...	**Bxc3+**
6.	**bxc3**	**Ne7** (*111*)

Black is not concerned about 7. dxc5 because the move would collapse White's pawn structure (four pawns on the queen's side and every one isolated) and in any case he will have no difficulty recovering the pawn, as you can easily work out. However, Black does have a few problems. The defences on his king's side are frail and he may have difficulty developing his bishop effectively. The greatest danger however lies in the potential weakness of the black squares, a key positional theme in the French. White's queen's bishop could prove a menace along the a3–f8 diagonal. White's only weakness is his disorganised pawns and for this reason they will be the target of Black's attack. Remember constantly to monitor the board in this way – it is the features, good and bad, of a position that breed ideas.

In the above variation, since Black planned to take off the knight anyway, could he not have done so at once and then moved up the c-pawn? (4... Bxc3+; 5. bxc3, c5.)

What is the difference? It is now White's turn to move instead of Black's because he has not been obliged to play the unhelpful a3. Do not hurry an exchange; your opponent may waste a move to prompt you to do what you intend anyway! Of course, if he dissolves the pin by removing the pinned piece (by castling, say) then you will have to make an immediate decision on whether you want to exchange or not – the knight may have gone next move.

140 *How Pieces Perish*

You saw above how a bishop could be ambushed by pawns. We return to the Ruy Lopez for another example.

This is an opening trap called the Noah's Ark on account of its antiquity, not because King Kong has a habit of falling into it.

	WHITE	BLACK
1.	e4	e5
2.	Nf3	Nc6
3.	Bb5	a6
4.	Ba4	d6
5.	d4	b5
6.	Bb3	Nxd4
7.	Nxd4	exd4 (*112*)

Now the pawn must not be taken at once. Best is 8. Bd5.

8.	Qxd4?	c5
9.	Qd5	Be6

Defending the mate and the rook simultaneously as well as attacking the queen – what could be called a useful move.

10.	Qc6+	Bd7
11.	Qd5	c4 (*113*)

The bishop is lost for two pawns.

It is rare for a knight to be deprived of an escape route unless it walks too far. There is a situation common to a number of openings where, if it strays to the side of the board, it can fall victim to a pawn.

Go back to (*89*). In this position, were Black so foolish as to take his knight to h5, it would have nowhere to go after the reply g4 (*114*). Did you say that would weaken White's king's position? True, but you should be willing to suffer considerable damage for the advantage of an extra piece.

BLACK

WHITE

112

BLACK

WHITE

113

It is not only minor pieces that can be lured to destruction on an open board. We have previously seen that incautious forays with the queen can bring condign punishment. Sometimes the penalty can be severe.

	WHITE	BLACK
1.	d4	c5

The Benoni Defence – remember?

	WHITE	BLACK
2.	dxc5	Qa5+
3.	Nc3	Qxc5

You will recall that this way of recovering the pawn was not recommended.

	WHITE	BLACK
4.	e4	d6
5.	Nf3	g6
6.	Nd5	Bg7 (*115*)

You would think that the one pawn White cannot now move is the b-pawn because this would expose the rook to the black bishop; but . . .

WHITE

BLACK

114

BLACK

WHITE

115

BLACK

WHITE

116

| 7. | b4! | Qc6 |
| 8. | Bb5! (*116*) | |

Now 8 . . . Qxb5; allows the knight fork 9. Nc7+.

141

It is hardly to be wondered at that the novice is at times bewildered by the wealth of apparently conflicting advice he receives. He is told to play aggressively and his attack is condemned as premature; he develops his pieces imaginatively and is advised to play natural moves, so makes natural moves and is censured for playing routinely, he's admonished for bringing out his queen and for not doing so.

There are no absolutes of good play, only guidelines. Each position must be judged on its merits alone which is why it is so important to THINK at every move. (Well, at almost every move. Some players ponder the mandatory. If your king is in check and there is only one way of getting out of it, there is no excuse for not moving quickly; you can examine the consequences later.)

Here is an attack that doesn't come off.

	WHITE	BLACK
1.	c4	d6
2.	Nc3	g6
3.	g3	Bg7
4.	Bg2	e5
5.	d3	Ne7 (*117*)

This is an opening we haven't seen before but by now you should be neither surprised nor alarmed by the unfamiliar. Notice that White has command of the central white squares and Black has control of the black. Black's last move indicates that he plans an early f5. Notice that if White were now to pin this piece with Bg5, after 6 . . . h6; he could not withdraw to h4 because of the reply g5 – compare the continuation to (*109*). This is an option you surrender when you fianchetto a bishop.

6.	e4	0–0
7.	h4	Nd7
8.	h5	Nf6
9.	hxg6	fxg6 (*118*)

BLACK | WHITE

WHITE | BLACK

117 | 118

White has conducted a copy-book attack to open the rook's file – but where are the assault troops? Black has meanwhile got on with his development. The rule when exchanging pawns is to capture towards the centre. Black decided to make an exception here because he wants to open the bishop's file for the rook. A wise decision; if White carries on his plan logically by exchanging the defending bishop he comes to grief; 10.

Bh6, Bxh6; 11. Rxh6, Ng4; and now White has both rook and f-pawn attacked and can contemplate an unhappy future.

Before we leave (*118*), observe that the pawn skeleton creates good outposts for knights for White at d5 and Black at d4 – with one difference; because Black has not moved his c-pawn he can attack d5 at any time.

Here is another attack that fades:

	WHITE	BLACK
1.	e4	d6
2.	d4	g6
3.	Nc3	Bg7
4.	Be3	Nf6
5.	f3	c6

Preparing the advance of the b-pawn.

6.	Qd2	h5

Black wants to avoid the exchange of bishops but this is a wasted move since if he castles, White can still force the bishops off with Bh6.

7.	0–0–0	b5 (*119*)

Black's pawn formation would have given the old masters heartburn, thus do fashions change.

8.	Nge2	Qa5
9.	Nf4	b4

An unjustified attack: Black is dangerously behind in development.

10.	Nb1	Qxa2
11.	Qxb4 (*120*)	

Black's queen is out of play. Further, White is threatening 12. Nc3, Qa1+; 13. Kd2 and any attempt to save the lady by 13… a5 would prove fruitless: 14. Qb3, a4; Qb4 (always keeping guard on the b-pawn) and salvation for Black is out of sight. Of course, Black has a move first but the outlook is bleak.

After 10. Nb1, White is poised to play 11. a3 followed by axb4 for Black's b-pawn is now pinned.

BLACK   WHITE

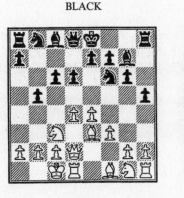   

WHITE   BLACK

119   120

142
Breaking the Rules

One of our two paramount principles is to play towards the centre and we stressed that knight moves to the side of the board are bad. Here is an opening where this, and one or two other maxims, are mutilated in the interests of tactical expediency.

	WHITE	BLACK
1.	e4	d5

This is known as the Centre Counter; an attempt by Black to get immediate equality. These first moves also occurred in our Cautionary Interlude.

2.   exd5

The logical reply. If Black now recaptures with the queen, he will have to move her again after 2. Nc3.

2.   ...   Nf6
3.   d4

You will find it hard to see why White does not keep the pawn he has won with 3. c4. The reason is that after 3... c6; 4. dxc6, Nxc6 Black has excellent development and White's d-pawn is backward with little chance of advancing to d4. Black has a fine positional game for the pawn sacrificed.

3.   ...   Nxd5

WHITE   WHITE

BLACK   BLACK

121   122

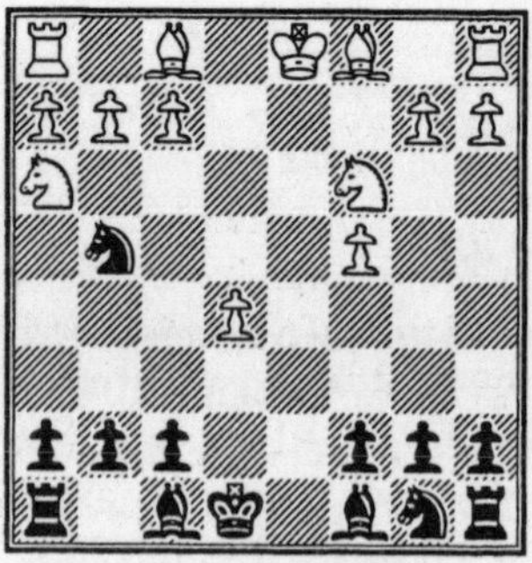

212

4.	c4	Nf6
5.	Nc3	e5 (*121*)

Black has made three moves with his knight, against the teaching, but White's centre now comes under attack.

6.	dxe5	Qxd1+
7.	Kxd1	

Foregoing the right to castle, but 7. Nxd1 would be a backward step and allow Black a time-gaining check with his bishop.

7.	...	Ng4

Threatening the fork of king and rook as well as the e-pawn.

8.	Nh3 (*122*)	

The best move to defend the f-pawn. A knight at h3 may later find a comfortable home at f4.

You will not have failed to comment that 8. f4 would simultaneously save the f-pawn and guard the e-pawn but would not prevent the fork. Did you also see that 8. Be3, Nxe3; 9. fxe3 leaves White with a wrecked pawn centre? Less obviously bad is 8. Ke1. The reason this is not good is that White, having forfeited the right to castle, will have difficulty activating his king's rook. If you cannot or do not wish to castle, the king may find safe haven at one of the second-rank squares where it will not impede the development of the rooks onto central files.

White could alternatively have played 8. Ne4 here but after 8... Bf5 he could not develop with 9. Bd3? on account of 9... Bxe4; 10. Bxe4, Nxf2+; followed by 11... Nxe4; and White has lost a piece.

8.	...	Nxe5
9.	Nb5	Na6 (*123*)

The same response! Black does not fancy 9... Bd6; 10. c5! (follow through the consequences of this move), nor 9... Kd8; surrendering the right to castle.

10.	Bf4	f6! (*124*)

Recall that this is generally a bad move in the opening, particularly true if the enemy queen is still on the board because of the open white diagonals near the king but recall also that a weakness is not a weakness if it cannot be exploited. Now if 11. Bxe5, fxe5; f4 is denied to the king's knight.

WHITE   BLACK

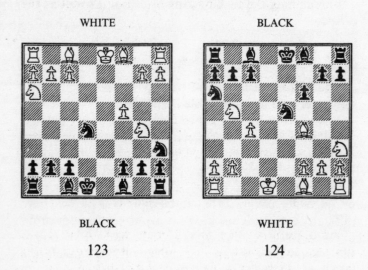

BLACK   WHITE

123   124

Of course, the black knight cannot move without losing the c-pawn while 10... Bd6; 11. Nxd6+, cxd6 would leave Black with a weak d-pawn. The text destroys White's hopes. Now Black will drive the knight back with c6, so White's 9th move was a vain sortie.

A tactical poser that crops up frequently is exemplified in the position. Black is at liberty to play Bxh3, ruining White's pawn formation on the king's side. If this were in front of a castled king, it would probably be a good idea but where it is not is another matter. Here, for example, Black would be ceding the advantage of the two bishops in order to remove a piece that has nowhere useful to go anyway; further, the move would grant White use of the open g-file for his rook. On balance, a bad exchange.

143   *Outlook Unpredictable*

It is not unusual for a stormy opening to settle into a tranquil middle game, nor for a placid start to turn wild.

	WHITE	BLACK
1.	d4	d5
2.	c4	e6
3.	Nc3	c6

A departure from the usual 3... Nf6. This passive-looking move takes away a good square from the knight but Black has planned compensation, as we shall see.

4.	Nf3	Nf6
5.	e3	Nbd7 (*125*)

As peaceful a scene as you could wish to see. Black appears to be putting his efforts into maintaining a pawn at d5 but this can hardly be the limit of his ambitions. Where does he go from here and what does he do about that buried bishop?

6.	Bd3	dxc4

We have seen this idea before: Black waits until White moves his king's bishop before capturing the c-pawn; thus forcing the piece to move again.

7.   Bxc4   b5

And again! True, Black has a bad pawn formation on the queen's side but this is only temporary. White must counter in the centre before Black gets too much space in which to manoeuvre. Witness the part played by Black's c-pawn.

8.   Bd3   a6

Black is preparing the advance 9... c5; which White cannot stop, opening a fine diagonal for the white-squared bishop.

9.   e4   c5
10. e5   cxd4
11. Nxb5 (*126*)

What will happen now? It's difficult to say because there are a number of plausible continuations. What is certain is that the game is at a critical stage just four moves after the first real contact between the forces.

The wary player expects the unexpected. When your opponent makes a move you have not considered, the first reaction is one of discomfort, if not alarm. It is possible the move is a crusher, but again it is possible that because you did not give it a thought, or your subconscious rejected it, it's a misjudgment. Look beyond the move to the idea behind it. That's good advice for any time, since it is often the coming rather than the immediate which is the danger.

144 *Knights and Bishops*

You have discovered that the most active pieces in the early moves of a game are the knights and bishops.

The text books tell you that these pieces are of approximately equal value, with the bishops preferred in open positions, where they are active, and the knights preferred in closed positions. Two bishops are usually favoured to a bishop and knight and almost always preferred to two knights, as we said earlier.

But these advantages are marginal, and it takes an expert to make use of them.

Bishops and knights may be of equal value but they do their own things. A bishop may move while retaining guard on a square, a knight cannot. A knight always alternates between black and white squares and can reach any square on the board whilst a bishop is restricted to half of them.

Have you noticed that when both sides are developed, it is quite usual for most of the pawns on one side to be on the opposite-coloured squares to those of the other? If, as suggested, you have been regarding the board as black with white squares and vice versa, you will have picked this up. This is especially true of openings like the French in which the pawn skeletons are locked together. Such formations have bearing on the values of the bishops. Unless the piece is vital for defence, be happy to exchange the bishop that is on the same colour as predominates in your pawn structure, particularly if confined behind it, but try to retain the bishop that is on the predominating colour of your opponent's pawn formation because it will be useful in offence.

We saw an example of an early exchange of bishop for knight in the Ruy Lopez: 1. e4, e5; 2. Nf3, Nc6; 3. Bb5, a6; 4. Bxc6, dxc6; (127).

White has given away the advantage of the two bishops. What has he got in return?

You are aware of the advantage of a passed pawn. It is the much-pursued prize in the end game when the vision of promotion brightens. White is already looking into the distance. Eventually, by playing d4, he will secure a pawn advantage on the king's side of 4 to 3 which should in time yield him a passed pawn.

When White's d-pawn departs, Black will have a queen's side majority also of 4–3. But Black has a doubled pawn on the c-file; his pawn formation is 'compromised'. Because of this, Black will not be able to achieve a passed pawn by force – leave all the pawns on the a-, b- and c-files, remove everything else from the board, and prove this to your satisfaction.

This of course is largely theoretical as there are going to be pieces moving around capturing things for a while yet, but nevertheless the pawn skeleton is in White's favour. And in passing, observe the colours of the squares of the two fixed central pawns – White has exchanged the right bishop.

Another example won't blunt your senses.

	WHITE	BLACK
1.	d4	Nf6
2.	c4	e6
3.	Nc3	Bb4

WHITE   WHITE

BLACK   BLACK

128   129

This is the Nimzo-Indian Defence. Now Black must be prepared to exchange bishop for knight if challenged at once or his move is purposeless.

| 4. | a3 | Bxc3 |
| 5. | bxc3 (*128*) | |

White has the two bishops but a slightly weakened pawn structure. Black has a choice of continuations based on different strategical ideas.

| 5. | ... | d6 |
| 6. | f3 | |

With Black's king's bishop departed, this move holds little danger and prepares the advance e4.

6.	...	0–0
7.	e4	e5
8.	Bg5 (*129*)	

145

This position deserves your attention.

White has built a powerful pawn centre but Black has got his pawns onto black squares so that his bishop has become good whereas White's king's bishop is, at least for the present, bad. Black should under no circumstances consider exd4 since this would not only undouble White's pawns but would render the strong White centre mobile.

White's pin of the knight is designed to embarrass Black. If the bishop is tickled with h6, it will retreat to h4, still keeping the pin. Black will be discouraged from expelling the bishop with g5 since this would weaken his king's position.

If Black had tried the same tactics on the queen's side, White would have been only too happy to continue the pursuit as this would gain a great deal of space at no danger. In fact, in this specific case, it would win a piece for a pawn: 1. d4, Nf6; 2. c4, e6; 3. Nc3, Bb4; 4. a3, Ba5?; 5. b4, Bb6; 6. c5 (*130*). No harm in another elementary reminder that in pursuit of strategical aims you should not neglect tactical truths!

Another sensible continuation from (*128*) runs:

| 5. | ... | c5 |

In order to fix White's pawn on c4 and perhaps later to attack it.

6.	e3	b6
7.	Bd3	Bb7
8.	f3	Nc6
9.	Ne2 (*131*)	

White has hastened castling and has temporarily immured his queen's bishop in order to give his king's

BLACK

131

bishop scope. His 8th move prevented occupation of his
e4 by a black piece and prepared the pawn move to e4.

Black has solved the problem of developing his
queen's bishop. True, the knight masks the bishop's line,

but it can move away at any time – and concealed attacks are often the most dangerous.

Having immobilised White's pawn on c4, Black might later attack it with advantage by Na5 and Ba6 coupled perhaps with d5.

146 *A Central Outpost*

A fianchettoed bishop puts pressure on the centre and can be a useful support for a knight outpost.

We saw in the last opening (*131*) how White developed his king's knight at e2 in order to stop occupation of his e4 by an enemy piece and to prepare the advance to e4, as in the previous example (*129*).

The black pawn skeleton (*131*) could equally have been reached from another line against 1. d4: the Queen's Indian Defence. This can come about when White avoids the Nimzo-Indian by bringing out his king's knight first. (Indian defences always involve bringing out bishops sideways: they got their name from the Indian game in which pawns are not allowed an initial two-step advance.)

	WHITE	BLACK
1.	d4	Nf6
2.	c4	e6
3.	Nf3	b6 (*132*)

Can you see Black's strategy? Because White has brought out his king's knight rather than his queen's knight, he cannot play e4 which would give him an advantage in the centre. Black intends to increase his grip on the square with the help of his queen's bishop.

4.	g3	Bb7
5.	Bg2	

132

One way to deal with a fianchetto on the queen's side is to counter it. We have seen how to deal with a fianchetto on the king's side in (*105*).

| 5. | ... | **Be7** |
| 6. | **0–0** | **0–0** (*133*) |

What is the significant difference between the two facing bishops? White's is guarded and Black's is not. That is a signal to watch out for tactical coups.

| 7. | **Nc3** | **Ne4** |
| 8. | **Qc2** | **Nxc3** |

Black always has to worry about this knight being pinned after White moves his king's knight.

| 9. | **Qxc3** | **f5** (*134*) |

Black has strengthened the e4 square and now plans d6, followed by Nd7 and an eventual e5. White also would

133   134

like to play e4 some time and can hasten this by moving his knight and exchanging the white-squared bishops.

Instead of taking the knight at once, White might have been tempted to try and exploit Black's unguarded bishop. Take back the last move on each side and play:

9. Ng5? (*135*)

At first glance, this looks a winner for it threatens mate as well as the undefended bishop. If now 9... Bxg5? 10. Bxb7 and not only is Black's rook under attack but his knight has no escape.

Unfortunately for White, Black has a stunning counter blow: 9 . . . Nxe2+! Now if White replies 10. Qxe2, Black continues 10 . . . Bxg2 and White will end up a piece down however he plays while 10. Kh1, Bxg2+ is rather worse!

Black has retained his king's bishop, unlike in the exchange variation of the Nimzo-Indian we examined. He could have exchanged it had he wanted. Continue from (*132*).

WHITE   WHITE

135   136

4.	g3	Bb7
5.	Bg2	Bb4+
6.	Bd2	Bxd2+
7.	Qxd2 (*136*)	

A technicality. White plans a possible d5 so wants his knight at c3 even though it means moving the queen again.

7.	...	0–0
8.	Nc3	Ne4
9.	Qc2	

9. Nxe4, Bxe4; allows Black equality as White's attacking chances have disappeared.

9.	...	Nxc3?
10.	Ng5! (*137*)	

Now the trap works. Black will lose rook for bishop: 10 . . . Qxg5; 11. Bxb7, Nxe2 (otherwise the knight will

be taken for nothing); 12. Qxe2 (12. Kxe2 would allow 12 . . . Nc6 and White has nothing better than 13. Bxc6 on account of the threatened fork of king and queen) Nc6; 13. Bxa8. Notice that Black's 12th move was imperative to avoid losing the rook for nothing. Black now has nothing better than 13 . . . Rxa8; when White is left with the advantage of rook against knight and pawn. Black might be tempted to delay the capture of the bishop by picking up another pawn and threatening the queen with 13 . . . Nxd4. But that would be a mistake as the knight is then undefended (always a danger, remember?) so White could play for example 14. Qe4, simultaneously attacking the knight and defending the bishop to emerge with the bigger advantage of rook against two pawns.

147   *Breaking the Rules Again*

Contradictions are common in the openings. A good example is Alekhine's Defence where Black brings out a knight, then moves it again – and again. This affront to principles is justified in our equation of give-and-take. Black entices White to advance his centre pawns and then sets about demolishing them – or, at least, trying to. The struggle is finely balanced: White has the advantage of space in which to manoeuvre but, as we have seen, advanced pawns can prove weak in the end game – if they don't collapse earlier. Black loses time and gets a cramped position, but that may only be temporary.

	WHITE	BLACK
1.	e4	Nf6
2.	e5	Nd5
3.	c4	Nb6
4.	d4 *(138)*	

As unorthodox an opening as you could wish for! White has a fine centre – but can it be maintained? Compare *A Pawn Charge (92)*.

4.	...	d6
5.	f4	

After 5. Nf3, Bg4 White will be under some pressure.

5.	...	dxe5
6.	fxe5	Nc6 *(139)*

Compare *(139)* below. Things are looking a little different now! You can see that Black is threatening N or Qxd4 but White cannot advance the pawn because of Nxe5. That would be a tactical error. What do you think of 7. c5? A positional error. The knight will return to d5 and a black piece will hold the square henceforth; White's centre pawns will be paralysed. At that point, experts would declare the game positionally lost for White.

7.	Be3	Bf5

8.	Nc3	e6
9.	Nf3 (*140*)	

Black must prepare against the advance d5, otherwise White's centre could become overwhelming.

9.	...	Bb4
10.	Be2	0–0
11.	0–0 (*141*)	

Lo! Despite the irregular start, we have model development: all the knights and bishops are out and both sides have castled. White still has the powerful pawn centre and now also has an open file for his king's rook. Black must disrupt the centre soon. He might try 11. . . Bxc3. This would bring two small benefits; it will discourage the advance d5 because it has removed a White guard on that square, and it doubles White's pawns on the c-file where they could become targets of attack.

BLACK   WHITE

WHITE   BLACK

140   141

148
An Exercise in Logic

As a break from all that theory which has probably got your head swimming, here is a little game that does not get beyond the opening. It was actually played in a match. White's reasoning, lettered for reference, is given after each Black move. Sometimes the logic is sound, sometimes it is flawed. Can you fault it and suggest improvements for White without sneaking a glance at the subsequent play? If you don't trust yourself, cover the page with a sheet of paper and move it down as you progress.

	WHITE	BLACK
1.	d4	d5

(a) This offer of a pawn hardly assists Black's development. Anyway, if I don't take it Black gets instant equality in the centre.

| 2. | dxe5 | Nc6 |

(b) The pawn is under attack. I can defend it in four ways. 3. f4 weakens the king's position: 3 . . . Bc5; might prove a bit embarrassing. 3. Bf4 breaks a well-honoured opening maxim: develop knights before bishops. 3. Qd5 must be wrong since Black can develop with 3 . . . Ng7 followed, when the queen moves, with Ng6, attacking the pawn a second time. Developing a knight with a step towards castling seems the best.

| 3. | Nf3 | Qe7 |

(c) Black's move must be weak: it brings out the queen too early and in particular obstructs the development of his king's side pieces. However, the pawn is again attacked and if I allow it to be captured my advantage will vanish. There are two ways to defend it, with the queen or the bishop; also I could counter-attack with 4. Bg5 but then after 4... f6; my pawn would disappear and Black would be ahead in development though I would be a pawn up. On balance, I favour a solid defence.

| 4. | Bf4 | Qb4+ (*142*) |

(d) This is a triple attack, on my king, bishop and b-pawn. Since I don't want to lose a piece for nothing, only two moves can be considered: Qd2 or Bd2. 5. Qd2 must be wrong, because after 5... Qxb2; 6. Qc3 (the only way to save the rook), Bb4 will win the queen for bishop. So I must bring the bishop back – fortunately it is not now needed to guard the pawn.

| 5. | Bd2 | Qxb2 |

(e) True, Black has got his material back and is threatening my rook and e-pawn simultaneously, but I can defend both of these and attack the queen also, forcing her to move once again.

6.	Bc3	Bb4

(f) The rook is once more attacked because the bishop is pinned. If I continue 7. Bxb4, Black need not take the rook. He can recapture 7... Nxb4 with the rook still under attack and the only way I can get out of that is to give up a piece by 8. Na3, but even that won't be the end of my troubles. My only resource seems to be Qd2, when I will lose rook for bishop after 7 ... Qxa1; 8. Bxa1, Bxd2+; however, I shall have a strong centre pawn, a powerful black-square bishop and the better development – good compensation.

7.	Qd2	Bxc3

(g) Of course, if 8. Nxc3, Qxa1+ will leave Black a whole rook ahead.

8.	Qxc3	Qc1 mate *(143)*

(h) (White's comment here is unrecorded.)

Let's now return to the reasoning and see where White went wrong.

Is (a) correct? Certainly: Black's first move is a gift depriving his king's knight of its best square. No other white move is worth more than a moment's thought.

The logic of (b) is equally valid. The first sentence of (c) is a fair assessment but thereafter the reasoning falters. White could simply develop now with 4. Nc3 and is well in front because of the badly placed queen. The alternative of 4. Bg5 must be evaluated. Black would not continue 4 ... f6; 5. exf6, but 4 ... Qb4+ as in the game. Now the bishop is not attacked, allowing White to avoid disaster with 5. Nbd2, but after 5 ... Qxb2, Black is

WHITE   WHITE

142   143

again threatening the advanced pawn as well as Nb4; so White will lose another pawn at least. Better still might be 5. Bd2, as in the game, but we'll consider that shortly.

Now that the black queen has denied e7 to the king's knight, 4. Qd5 is worth inspection. Because his queen's bishop still guards the b-pawn, White can answer 4 . . . Qb4+, with 5. Nc3 or 5. c3. The knight advance 4 . . . Nb4, threatening both the queen and the fork of king and rook, would be a clear case of a wasted move. White has only to bring the queen back to b3 and the knight would soon be compelled to resume his travels. Black has nothing better than 4 . . . f6 in response to 4. Qd5, when after 5. exf6, Nxf6; the white queen may do best to go home. The extra pawn yields White a decided advantage.

Comment (d) is fair: 5. Bd2 is White's best move here. The logic in (e) is evidently false in the light of subsequent play. White has in fact a perfectly good reply to 5 . . . Qxb2; in 6. Nc3 (*144*).

This move is usually the best in situations of this kind. Play might continue: 6 . . . Bb4; 7. Rb1, Qa3; 8.

BLACK

WHITE

144

WHITE

BLACK

145

WHITE

BLACK

146

Rb3, Qa5. Does this strike a chord? Look back at (*100*). Now White gets a fine game with 9. a3.

No less difficult for Black is 6 ... Nb4; 7. Nd4 (to guard against the knight fork), Bc5 (to break the guard); 8. Rb1, Qa3 (now the knight fork is no longer a threat); 9. Nb3 (*145*).

Black's bishop is under attack and he will have difficulty extricating his queen. If the bishop goes back to b6 (9 ... Bb6) White has the pretty 10. Bc1 and Black must give up his knight (10... Nxc2+) to allow the queen to escape. Look also for good White continuations after 9 ... Be7; or 9 ... Nc6; or 9 ... Nxa2. No answers: you are meant to be getting the ideas now!

The retreat 10 ... Qa6 is met with 11. e3 and the queen has nowhere to go (*146*). If White plays carelessly 11. e4? Black has 11 ... Bxf2+ and the queen (but not much else) survives. Black could try desperately 11 ... Nxa2 and you would reply ... ?

Comment (f) is all right except for the faulty reasoning in the last sentence.

Comment (g) is correct but the alternative proves fatal.

149

Chess players at all levels are subject to blunders, the result of temporary blindness. There is no known prophylactic but you can stop the disease reaching epidemic proportions by a little self-discipline. One precaution you can take is to draw up a brief check-list which you run through before making each move. Nothing elaborate: something that absorbs just a few seconds of thought.

First, you must identify the main causes of your blunders. These are likely to include overlooking checks, unguarded men, threats – for example, masked attacks – and simple exchanges that destroy a guard. Put them together in a mnemonic and you are in practice.

You could try the doubly-appropriate CHECK, where C stands for Captures, H for Hazards, E for

Exposure, C for Centre and K for King. So first you look at the immediate consequences of all possible captures. Then under H you examine for threats, particularly arising from your opponent's last move. Exposure is undefended men – are they in danger? The Centre is a prime concern in the opening – is anything eventful about to happen? Collapse? Rigor mortis? Finally, the king. Look at all possible checks, including those involving sacrifices. You know why checks are important: they severely limit your choice of moves.

That's just an idea for a check-list. You'll be able to think up something better for yourself.

150   *A Useful Study*

Now as a finale (you have openings coming out of your ears?) there is a useful little study that will serve you well as it is difficult to think of an opening in which it doesn't occur. This is the pin of a knight either against the king or the queen by a bishop.

It is enough that you know the objects of each side in this small battle within a battle, and the usual alternatives that may be available. An understanding of these will lead you to the correct way to deal with less common positions.

Each knight on its first play may have a choice of up to three squares to which to move. Let us take, as an example, White's QN. One square is at the edge of the board (a3), and two are towards the centre (c3 and d2). The move away from the centre (Na3) is almost always bad, and of the other two, Nc3, which strikes at two central squares, is usually best. However, a knight whose initial move is to the c- or f-file can often be pinned against the king or queen respectively. The pin of a knight by a bishop under these circumstances can favour the attacker in several small ways:

(*a*) The move develops a piece (the bishop);

(*b*) The pin at once stops an enemy piece (the knight) from moving and temporarily destroys its powers;

(*c*) The pin often hinders enemy development;

(*d*) The attack frequently threatens to gain a positional advantage, and sometimes to win material. For this reason the pin may compel a reply which is defensive or otherwise not the best.

Against these advantages must be set the fact that the pin often threatens nothing or makes only a temporary weakness in the enemy position. The bishop may then be driven away or forced to take the knight, in both cases with probable loss of time. In sum, the pin is often, but by no means always good.

151

Let us look first at the most serious threat: gain of material. Here the idea is the same that we saw in **47** *D*. If the knight can be attacked with a pawn, the piece may be lost. *A* shows part of an opening position. The knight cannot be saved. A more common position, which at first sight also loses a piece, is shown in *B*. Notice the difference between *A* and *B*. Now Black, to play, can save the piece at the cost of a pawn by attacking the bishop (*C*).

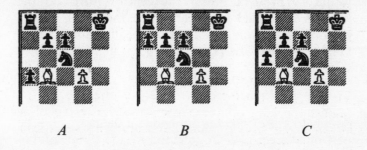

A   *B*   *C*

If the bishop moves back to keep the pin, Black attacks it again with the knight's pawn. However White plays he cannot do better than win a pawn. Positions similar to these will recur many times in your openings: look closely at them!

152

Consider now the two types of opening pin; against the king where the knight cannot legally move, and against the queen where it may move but probably only at great loss (*A*). White would not wish to capture the king's knight in *A* because this would help Black's development and leave his pawns undisturbed.

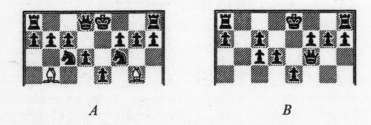

A   *B*

The position is different on the queen's side. If the bishop took the knight here, Black would be forced to double his pawns and isolate his rook's pawn, thereby making weaknesses in the pawn structure (**71**). The exchange would favour Black, however, in that a pawn would be brought nearer the centre (**74B**) and the knight's file would be open for the rook (**76**); also, a bishop is normally worth just a shade more than a knight. *B* shows the position if both of these captures were made.

153

Simply to pin a knight is not enough: the move must be part of a larger plan. A common idea is an advance in the centre which the pinned knight cannot prevent. *A* and *B* show this idea in its simplest form: in both positions White is free to advance the rear pawn to secure an aggressive pawn centre. Another possibility is piece play against the weak knight. *C* shows it under attack from a second man, a white knight. Now White can wreck Black's pawn position by capturing with either piece since Black would have to recapture with the pawn or lose his queen. A typical continuation for White after the exchange of knights would be an attack against the rook (*D*).

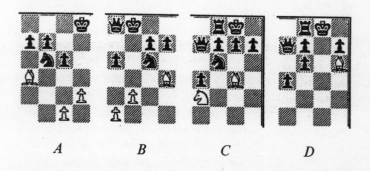

A   *B*   *C*   *D*

The main danger here is not to the rook (which can move away) but to the king who now stands open to attack.

As Black cannot at once escape the situation in *C*, White may do better to delay the capture of the knight. Do not be in a hurry to seize an opportunity that will still be available next move.

154

Fighting the Pin

Now consider the pin from the defender's viewpoint. A common idea is to attack the bishop at once with the rook's pawn (*A*), forcing it either to capture the knight or to try to keep the pin by moving back a square. This pawn move has the additional advantage of allowing the king an escape square against the possibility of a mating threat on the back rank later on.

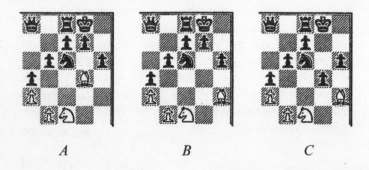

A   *B*   *C*

If the attacker retreats, let us consider this new position (*B*). At any time Black now has the option of moving up his knight's pawn two squares, attacking the bishop and at the same time freeing the knight from the pin (*C*). This second advance may or may not be good for, although forcing the bishop off the diagonal, it will likely weaken the pawn position. This could be a very dangerous manoeuvre on the same side as the castled king, as here.

The one-square move of the rook's pawn is frequently played in the opening to stop an embarrassing pin; but the move should not be freely used as it is rather too peaceful – it is sometimes called the 'country move!' These same ideas are seen where the knight is pinned against the king, though here the attack may be less strong since the action will be on the queen's side and the king will probably castle on the other wing.

There are several ways in which a defender may free himself from a pin and yet prevent his pawn wall from being broken. Let us consider the case where the knight is pinned against the queen (*A*). Here White can unpin the knight by playing his queen up two squares (*B*). As the queen still defends the knight, Black cannot double

the white pawns by exchanging. In *C*, the pin is released
by a bishop move. Another defence is to play the second
knight to guard his companion (*D*): this does not free
the pin at once but does permit the queen to move where
she pleases without allowing the pawns to be broken.

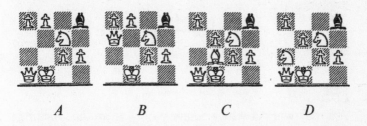

| A | B | C | D |

Where the knight is pinned against the king we have
these same ideas to prevent the break-up of the pawns.
The king can then be moved to safety, ideally by castling. If there is a risk that the exchange of bishop for
knight will weaken the pawn position, it is important to
castle on the opposite side of the board otherwise the
king may be open to attack.

PART SEVEN

The End Game

155

You may wonder why we have passed from the Opening to the End Game, leaving out the Middle Game.

The middle game is the battle proper in which you have to find your own way helped by a few guiding principles and your own experience. We have already studied these principles in the Parts on Tactics and, particularly, Strategy. The opening and the end game, on the other hand, lend themselves to study. If you start the game well, you will enter the middle game with confidence and if you understand the end game you will be confident of where you are going in the middle game.

156

The end game may be described as that stage of the game in which both sides are so reduced in forces as to be unable to win by direct attack. A typical end game might have on the board, apart from the kings, one or two pieces and a number of pawns on each side. Although the end game comes at the end of a game, not all games have an end game: some finish in the middle game or even, as we saw in Part Six, in the opening. Also, end games can be very long – sometimes longer than the opening and middle game together.

157

There are other features of the end game. Because the forces are reduced, so is the danger to the kings who can now become active, fighting pieces. For the same reason, the value of the remaining pawns is greatly increased as prospects for promotion are much brighter. Both sides, too, have more space to move about in, which often means that there is a wider choice of plans than there is in the middle game. This does not mean a wider choice of good plans; usually there is only one good plan in an ending.

The skills you need to know for the end game can be reduced to two:

(a) Promoting a pawn.
(b) Mating with a small force.

158

Of course, the end game is not as easy as that, in fact it is probably the most difficult part of chess, but these are the two skills that will be in most demand.

In the end game, because of the few men engaged, the same kinds of positions recur many times. It is for this reason that the end game, like the opening but unlike the middle game, has been deeply studied. The correct ways to handle different types of ending have been developed over many years, even centuries, so that today much hard thinking is saved for us; which does not mean that memory is enough, for in the end game, as in all chess, understanding is the first essential. It is not even enough to play the right moves: they must also be played in the right order.

159   *King and Pawn v. King*

The ending of king and pawn against king is not only a common one, it is a basic one. Any game in which one side is a pawn ahead can, in theory, be reduced by exchanges to this three-man battle. With a bigger material advantage of course, the stronger side should find his problems easier.

The elements of this ending are not difficult. No checkmate is possible with king and pawn against king: set the three men on the board and try and construct a mating position with them and you will see that it cannot be done. For the stronger side to win it is therefore necessary to promote the pawn.

The defence by the solitary king is first to try to capture the pawn. If the other king cannot interfere, there is a simple way to decide whether or not a pawn can be caught.

Look at *A* and imagine a 'magic square', one side being the distance from the square on which the pawn stands to its queening square, the other of course the same distance along the rank. As the pawn advances, this 'magic square' is reduced in size. The rule is that the opposing king can catch the pawn if he is within the 'magic square' or can enter it.

A　　　　　　　*B*

If the pawn is on its starting square (*B*), do not forget to allow for the initial double move. In both examples, Black, with the move, can catch the pawn, but if White moves first the pawn will safely queen.

160

If the pawn can be defended, then the lone king should try to place himself in its path. Unless he now gives way the pawn is unable to queen and the game is therefore drawn. However, there are several positions where the lone king can be forced aside by the opposing king. This 'battle of the kings' is an important part of king and pawn endings, though really it is more like a ballet than a battle as the kings cannot, as we know, attack each other. Frequently, however, they approach each other; if the two kings stand face to face with one square between them, the king that moves first has to give way. Neither king can advance in diagram *A*. Let us suppose that the black king must move (*B*), then the white king can go forward one rank (*C*). Now the black king can also move down one rank (*D*) but again the white king can go forward (*E*) and you will see that White is a move ahead. This extra move is often vital in the end game where the first player to promote a pawn usually wins. Any other move for the black king in *A* would be at least as bad as that played.

A   *B*   *C*   *D*   *E*

161

Why are king moves so important? Look at *A*. White's pawn is two steps from becoming a queen and the kings are facing each other: there are no other pieces on the board. If White moves first, he can only draw, but if Black is to play, White wins. Follow the play carefully for this small battle will occur many times in your end games.

A　　　*B*　　　*C*　　　*D*　　　*E*

If White advances the pawn, giving check, the black king will move in front of it (*B*). What is White to do? He cannot move the pawn again, and if he moves the king to keep guard on it, the black king is stalemated (*C*). Any other move of the white king will allow Black to capture the pawn.

Alternatively, White can, in *A*, move his king to any of four squares (these are not included in the miniboard but may be easily imagined), but the black king can then move in front of the pawn and White can make no progress.

The game is a draw as White cannot promote the pawn.

If Black moves first he must place his king in front of the pawn. White now advances the pawn and the position in *B* is again reached but this time with Black to play. There is only one move (*D*), when White can play up his king (*E*) and the pawn will be safely queened next move. The mate of king and queen against king is then easily forced, as we shall see.

162

This is a striking example of what is called the OPPOSITION – a situation where the two kings face each other. The side who is forced to move his king is said *not* to have the opposition. Notice that the positions of the kings in **161** *A* and *E* correspond to their positions in **160** *A* and *D*.

It is possible to have also a *diagonal opposition* (the kings on the same diagonal with one square between them) and a *distant opposition*, when the kings are farther apart. It is often a winning advantage to have the opposition in king and pawn end games. If there are pieces on the board as well, however, the opposition may be of little or no importance.

163

Let us now inspect other possible endings of king and pawn against king where the pawn is supported and the defender can get his king ahead of the pawn on the same file. *In the case of a rook's pawn the game is a draw whoever has the move.* Look at *A*. Here we have **161***A* again but at the edge of the board. If Black is to move, he goes into the corner and the pawn advances (*B*) – White can make no headway with king moves. Now we have position **161***B* again except, because the black king is on the rook's file, he cannot be forced to move out on the other side of the pawn. The position is stalemate.

A   B   C   D   E

Even if a defender cannot reach the rook's file, the ending is still often drawn. Look at *C*. The game is drawn whoever moves first. If White moves, he must play up his king and Black moves to keep the opposition (*D*) although he could also draw here by attacking the pawn. Now if White advances the pawn it is his turn to be stalemated. If Black moves first, White does no better. If he moves his king back to free his pawn (*E*) the black king goes to the knight's file and we have the draw shown in *A*.

164

In cases where the pawn is not a rook's pawn and the defending king can reach the queening square of the pawn, the attacker will win if his king is two or more squares ahead of his pawn because he can always use a pawn move to get the opposition. Where the attacker's king is one square in front or level with his pawn, he may win if he has the opposition.

165

With several pawns on the board in addition to the kings, the player who has more usually wins. The aim of the stronger side in these cases is to force a passed pawn or to exchange pawns until a won K & P *v.* K ending is reached.

Where both sides have the same number of pawns, the player whose king is better placed can sometimes win. These remarks refer to positions in which the pawn formations are *uncompromised*; that is, those that do not include doubled or backward pawns. See diagram *A*. Here White has an uncompromised pawn majority on the king's side and so can force a passed pawn by playing up his rook's pawn two squares. Whether or not Black now exchanges pawns, the black king will be outside the 'magic square'. If Black plays first in *A*, however, he advances his pawn and the white pawn majority is compromised since the rook's pawn is backward (*B*). In fact, White would now lose quickly for since his king cannot move, he must play up his rook's pawn. Whether it is moved one square or two, Black will capture it (don't forget 'en passant' – **24**). Now the second white pawn can move so there is no stalemate. The black pawn promotes to queen at the same time giving checkmate.

A   *B*

If, in position *A*, the men on the left-hand side had all been one square over to the right, White, with the move, could only have drawn as the black king would have been able to move inside the 'magic square'. This would have allowed the white king to capture the black pawn next to him and both sides would have been left with bare kings.

166

It is quite common with equal pawns to find majorities on opposite wings. Thus in **165** above White has a pawn extra on the king's side, Black on the queen's side. It is also common in endings to find the kings near to each other. Where these situations occur (pawns unbalanced, kings together), again as in **165**, it is favourable to have the pawn majority on the side away from the kings – and the farther away the better. This is true whether or not there are pieces on the board and it is one of those points you should bear in mind when exchanging men in the late middle game.

167

Stopping Pawn Promotion

The first defensive duty of a piece in the end game (apart from preventing checkmate) is to stop enemy pawns promoting. The action necessary against a passed pawn takes one of three forms. These are, in preferred order:

(*a*) Capture the pawn;
(*b*) Stop the pawn advancing by attacking a square in its path (as in **72F**);
(*c*) Sacrifice the piece for the pawn if it will otherwise queen.

It is not, of course, possible to sacrifice the king to stop a pawn promoting and it would be pointless to give up the queen for this purpose, but these are the only exceptions.

168

A single, unsupported pawn whose path is clear is easily captured by king, queen or rook, but it can always escape capture by a bishop or a knight by moving ahead when it is attacked. A minor piece should therefore be moved not to attack the pawn but to attack a square in front of it. If this is not entirely clear to you it would be wise to work it out on a board.

169

If one pawn is easily stopped, two pawns together need care. If the pawns are far from promotion the task of the pieces is not hard. In *A*, *B* and *C* the pawns are held whichever side moves. If White has no move elsewhere on the board, then both pawns are lost in each case. Play these through: you will find that the advanced pawn must be attacked in *C*.

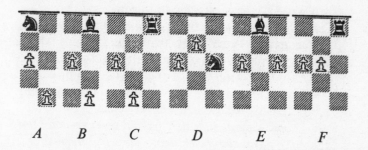

A   *B*   *C*   *D*   *E*   *F*

If the pawns are farther advanced, it may not be possible to stop one of them queening. In the next three examples (*D, E* and *F*) the pieces are helpless whichever side moves first. White gives up a pawn to promote the other in each case. Again, you would do well to work these out.

170

The queen deals easily with several pawns and the king too can stop a pair of passed pawns even if they are far advanced. *A* shows such a situation. The pawns cannot get through however White plays – the king even has a choice of squares. *B, C* and *D* are three possible continuations. The king is always free to move and keep

A   *B*   *C*   *D*   *E*

guard on the pawns but he can never take the rear pawn without allowing the other to queen. This is a common grouping which may occur anywhere on the board: the pawns are safe from attack by the king but cannot force their way past. If the white king arrives to help however, a pawn will have easy passage to queen.

It is curious that sometimes two isolated pawns can present a greater threat than two united pawns which are otherwise much stronger. In *E*, the king is unable to move without allowing one of the pawns to promote.

If White is forced to move in any of the positions *B–E*, both pawns will be lost in every case.

It is a good general rule that passed pawns should not be allowed to advance further than necessary: the nearer a pawn is to queen, the greater is the danger for the defence.

171

Minor Piece Endings

In the ending king and minor piece against king and one or more pawns, the player with the piece cannot win. He should try and capture the pawn(s), giving up the piece if necessary, in order to draw.

172

In the ending king, minor piece and pawn against bare king the stronger side always wins with one important exception. *A rook's pawn and a bishop not of the same colour as the queening square of the pawn can only draw where the defending king can reach the queening square.* This ending is more common than you might imagine. In *A* you will see that whoever moves, White can neither mate nor force the pawn through.

Where both sides have a minor piece and pawns, the side with the most pawns should usually win but again there is an exception and again this involves the bishop on account of its one-colour move. *If both sides have one bishop, and they are on opposite-coloured squares, then even an advantage of two pawns may not be enough to win. B* and *C* illustrate this: the weaker side takes control of the squares of one colour and the stronger side can do nothing to improve his position.

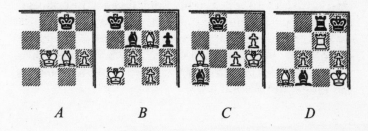

A   B   C   D

The *bishops of opposite colour* (as these are called) have an important part in the game. As the end game approaches, or even earlier, the weaker side may play to obtain them in the hope of eventually reaching a position similar to *B* or *C*. This is an idea which can be missed in the general battle. Look at *D*. Black is badly placed for he is two pawns behind; however, the right bishops are there and he has only to exchange the rooks to draw.

If other pieces are on the board as well as the bishops, and these pieces cannot be easily exchanged, then the opposite-colour bishops may be of no help to the weaker side.

173

Where each side has only a bishop left, apart from pawns, but the bishops are on the same coloured squares, then the better-placed side will sometimes win even if the forces are level.

174

A great deal could be written about the bishop *v.* knight duel in the end game. In general, a knight is best in a close position and where it can attack weak squares of both colours (though not of course at the same time). A bishop is better where there are pawns on both sides of the board. Sometimes a bishop can contain (that is, limit the movement of) a knight, as in *A*, and sometimes it is the knight who can contain the bishop (*B*). When a minor piece can be trapped, like the knight in *A*, it is often possible simply to walk up the king and take it.

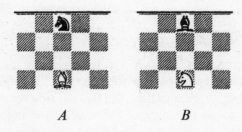

A   *B*

175

An advantage that the bishop has over the knight is that it can usually 'lose' a move, which the knight cannot. In *A*, White plays up the bishop one square, stopping the black pawn from moving and keeping guard on the queening square of the white pawn. Now the knight must move and the pawn will queen.

There is an important idea in this ending also – the 'good' and 'bad' bishop (77). The bishop is 'good' in *B* for it is on the same-coloured squares as the enemy pawns. A sacrifice quickly decides the game: 1. Bxg6 ch! and White will queen a pawn however Black plays. An example of a 'bad' bishop is shown in *C*. White wins by bringing the king up (always a sound idea in the end game if there is no obvious play). 1. Ka6. Now if Black checks, White reaches a won pawn ending: 1... Bc8+; 2. Nxc8, Kxc8; 3. Kb6, Kd7; 4. Kb7 (the opposition!). The pawn is now lost and White will force a queen. Note these king moves: this is a common winning strategy where one king is well advanced. If the black king moves away he fares no better: 1... Kd8; 2. Kb7, Ke7; 3. Kc7 and Black, with nothing attacked, is in zugzwang (**31**).

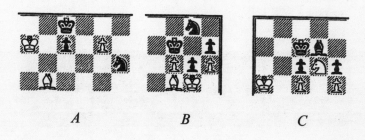

A   *B*   *C*

Like the 'opposite colour' bishops, the 'good' and 'bad' bishop are something to think about before the end game is reached.

176   *Rook and Pawn Endings*

Rook and pawn end games are the most common and often the most difficult. To play them well can take long study but we shall be content to keep our aims few and simple and to avoid the bad mistakes.

The first point to bear in mind is that king and rook alone can force mate against a bare king. Where one side has a rook and the other side a pawn only guarded by the king, the stronger side will always win if he can bring his king next to the pawn which can then be captured by the rook.

If the stronger side cannot do this, then the game is drawn because the rook will have to be given up for the pawn when it promotes to queen as the ending K & Q v. K & R is, with correct play, lost for the weaker side.

In *A*, White draws by advancing the pawn, but he must be careful in responding to rook checks. After 1. b6, Rc4+; 2. Kd8 (or d7 or d6), and if the rook checks again, the king must move back to the c-file. If the king moves too far from the pawn the rook will capture it, and if he moves in front of the pawn (for example, with 2. Kb7) Black will have time to bring his king back, and the pawn will fall.

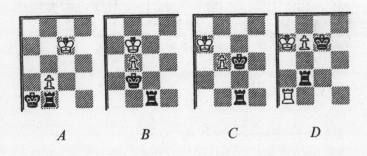

A   *B*   *C*   *D*

Study this second case as an example of the care that must be taken in a 'simple' ending like this one. After 1. b6, Rc4+; 2. Kb7?, Kb5 the position in *B* is reached. White plays 3. Ka7, preparing to advance the pawn. Black's best reply is Kc6 as this forces mate sooner, though he could also play 3... Ra4+; 4. Kb7, Ra6 and the pawn is lost next move.

After 3... Kc6 White has only a choice of losing moves. Let us *analyse* the ending from here on (that is, consider every possibility), not because it is an important ending but simply as an exercise in 'chess thinking'. From position *C* then, we will examine each line of play based on White's move at this point.

(*a*) 1. Ka6, Ra4 mate	(*d*) 1. b7, Ra4+;
	2. Kb8, Rb4;
	3. Ka8, Kc7;
	(note 3... Rxb7?
	stalemate!)
(*b*) 1. Kb8, Kxb6;	4. b8(Q)+, Rxb8+;
2. Ka8, Rc8 mate	5. Ka7, Rb6;
	6. Ka8, Ra6 mate

or

3. Kc8, Rxb7;
4. Kd8, Kd6;
5. Ke8, Ra7;
6. Kf8, Ke6;

(*c*) 1. Ka8, Kxb6;   7. Kg8, Kf6;
      2. Kb8, Rc5;   8. Kh8, Kg6;
      3. Ka8, Rc8 mate   9. Kg8, Ra8 mate

The basic case in rook and pawn endings is rook and one pawn against rook. The rule here is that if the defending king can move in front of the pawn the game is almost always drawn (similar, you will notice, to a K & P *v.* K ending). The winning method for the stronger side is to get his king guarding the promotion square and sheltered from checks by using his own rook as an umbrella (*D* above). In this example, White can win in two ways, by checking with the rook to drive the king away and then promoting the pawn, or by promoting the pawn at once, allowing the black rook to take the newborn queen, and then checking the king so that it is driven away from the defence of the rook which will be captured by the white king.

177

A simple rule to remember in these endings is *rooks behind passed pawns*. This is true whether you are trying to promote your pawn or stop your opponent's pawn; it is also good advice for the middle game too!

In *A*, the black rook is behind the passed pawn and is therefore better placed than the white rook. You can see, for example, that the black rook can move up and down the rook's file and still keep watch on the advanced white pawn but the white rook is unable to move without leaving the pawn 'en prise'.

This is a drawn ending. If the white king moves up to defend the pawn in order to free the rook to allow the pawn to promote, the black rook can check him away and then return to the rook's file to keep the attack on the pawn.

Now consider *B*. Here we have the same position but with the rooks reversed with the white rook behind the pawn and the black rook in front of it. White wins easily by moving up his king when Black will have to give up his rook for the pawn or allow it to queen.

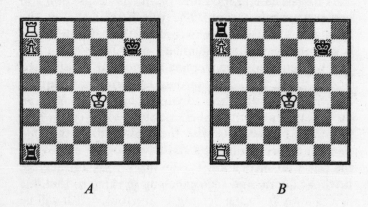

A   *B*

178

In rook and pawn endings where there is more than one pawn on the board and in many other endings we have not space to look at here, there are two ideas to keep in mind:

(*a*) The side that is ahead in material should normally win;

(*b*) The winning method for the stronger side is to reduce the position to one of the basic endings we have been looking at.

The stronger side can usually force the play as the weaker side is likely to have less choice of moves. An exchange or even a sacrifice may then be made at the right time.

179 *Queen and Pawn Endings*

In the king and queen *v.* king and pawn ending the stronger side has only to place his queen in front of the pawn and then to bring up his king to capture it. You will find that there is no way for the weaker side to force the queen aside as *the queen is the one piece that can never be approached by a king*.

The only position that gives a little difficulty is that where the pawn is already on the seventh rank and the promotion square is attacked by the king so that the queen cannot occupy it (*A*). White still wins from any position by reaching the situation shown in *B*. This he can easily do by a series of checks as the black king must guard the pawn and also stop the queen occupying the promotion square. Now the king must go in front of the pawn when the white king can be brought nearer. Black would then move his king away again threatening

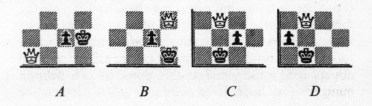

| A | B | C | D |

to promote and White would continue as before, forcing position *B* again. When the white king arrives next to the pawn, checkmate will quickly follow.

If the pawn on the seventh rank happens to be a bishop's or rook's pawn however, the weaker side can draw by a stalemate threat. *C* is a similar situation to *B* except that the pawn is on a bishop's file. Black to move here can play his king in the corner threatening to promote, and if the pawn is taken he is stalemated. Similarly in *D* with a rook's pawn. Here the king again goes into the corner and the queen must move away to avoid the stalemate. As in both *C* and *D* White will find no time to bring his king up, he must give the draw.

180

We have seen how to promote pawns in order to get the big material advantage to force checkmate against any defence, and also how to stop pawns queening. This is one of the two skills that are most needed in the end game. The second skill (look back to **157**) is how to checkmate with a small force when all the pawns have gone from the board.

A single pawn, if it can be promoted, is enough to win. However, a single knight or bishop, worth three pawns in our table of values, is not.

Try to set up a checkmate position using king and knight or bishop against king. You will discover that even with the lone king in the corner this cannot be done. With a king and rook against king, however, mate is not only possible but can always be forced. This is the minimum mating force and is a common ending among students. It would be a common ending among experts too if it were not so well known that the weaker side will always resign the game at this point (if not before), being without hope. King and rook against king can be said to be the most important of all chess endings – if you cannot mate when the enemy king is defenceless you will not win many games!

181

The method of winning is straightforward but needs some attention. *The plan, which is common to all piece endings, is to drive the king to the edge of the board and to checkmate him there.* This checkmate we saw in 58*B* and in 61*B*. You may like to refresh your memory by looking back at these examples before going on.

Now follow through the sequences of play which is the same wherever the rook and kings are on the board.

(*a*) The rook is played to a rank or file to act as a wall to prevent the lone king escaping towards the centre of the board. This rank or file will normally be the one next to that on which the enemy king stands.

(*b*) The other king is then brought up until the two kings face each other *with the stronger side to play* (see *A*). A check by the rook (*B*) will then force the king back a rank and this sequence is repeated until the black king is at the edge of the board where he is mated.

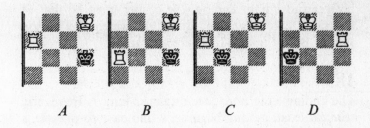

| *A* | *B* | *C* | *D* |

(*c*) The defender has two ways of delaying (but not avoiding) the mate. Firstly, by attacking the rook (*C*), when the correct play for White is to move the piece to the other side of the board *but staying on the same rank or file*. Secondly, by reaching a position similar to *A* with his (the defender's) turn to play. The right way to meet this manoeuvre may be to make a 'waiting' move with the rook, or to follow the lone king along with your king a knight's move away so that, when the edge of the board is reached (*D*), the enemy king will have to return opposite your king *when you have the move* (that is, position *A* again). A good example of this play was given in the second part of continuation (*d*) in the analysis in **176**.

In this ending, the defender will not move back towards the board edge unless he is forced to do so as this will simply make the attacker's job easier.

It would be well to practise this important ending until you have it 'move perfect' – but remember always to make the best moves for your opponent too!

182

There are two minor-piece endings in which mate can be forced: king, bishop and knight or king and two bishops against king. Both endings require that the bare king be driven into a corner of the board, and in the case of the bishop and knight ending, the corner must be that of the same colour as the square on which the bishop stands. Both these endings are very rare.

183

The ending king and queen against king is frequently seen (at least, among beginners) and easy to play. It is common because it often comes about from the promotion of the last pawn and is easy to play because the queen, being more powerful than the rook, can force back the enemy king quicker.

184

When attempting checkmate with a small force there is one comforting thought – a mistake (unless it is a very bad one) will not alter the result: the game will just go on a few more moves than was absolutely necessary. However, if you make too many small mistakes you may allow your opponent to escape with a draw under the fifty-move rule (**101**), so do not check around idly just because you have a solitary king to play with!

185

In all these endings the danger of a stalemate exists (and many players continue with only a king in the hope of just that). It is rare in the rook ending and can only occur when the king is in the corner; *A* and *B* are examples. In the case of the queen ending, however, the chance of stalemate is high. *C, D* and *E* are examples of which *C* is the most common.

The risk is also high in the minor piece endings *but in all cases the hunted king must be on the edge of the board for stalemate to occur*, so do not worry about this possibility too early!

| A | B | C | D | E |

186

A weaker force than king and rook cannot give checkmate. We have already seen that a king and bishop or king and knight cannot mate even with the help of the lone king.

Although mate can occur in the ending king and two knights against king, *it cannot be forced* and this ending is properly a draw also.

A larger material advantage – for example, king, queen and bishop against king – should give you no difficulty whatever if you have mastered the basic endings given. Only one warning here: the stronger the force, the greater the risk of stalemate. It is not unknown for the student, umpteen pieces up, to stalemate the bare king in a planless effort to capture him!

187

The most important features of the end game have now been explained and your understanding of them will serve you well for some time yet. Later you may want to refer to one of the several good books available that list and describe every type of ending you are ever likely to meet.

PART EIGHT

Games of the Masters

188

To give you an insight on how the world's top players battle against each other, here are the scores of six games played by chess masters past and present. They are in chronological order of date, and range from the swashbuckling era of a century and a half ago to the calculated aggression of modern play. All the games are decisive although in modern master play it is usual for more than half of all games to end in a draw. Treat these games as a spectacle; grand theatre to be observed and enjoyed. Do not attempt to study them in depth.

189   *King of the Classics*

This game, played in London in 1851 between two of the leading players of the day, is popularly known as the Immortal Game. Typically, both sides attack, with White sacrificing in turn both rooks, a bishop, and finally the queen.

	WHITE Anderssen	BLACK Kieseritzky
1.	e4	e5
2.	f4	exf4

The King's Gambit. White has given up a pawn to gain time and development.

| 3. | Bc4 | b5 |

Striking at the weak square f7. Black returns the pawn to deflect the bishop.

4.	Bxb5	Qh4+
5.	Kf1	Nf6
6.	Nf3	Qh6
7.	d3	Nh5
8.	Nh4	c6
9.	Nf5	Qg5
10.	g4	Nf6
11.	Rg1	cxb5

A sacrifice: the black queen now finds herself in a deal of trouble.

12.	h4	Qg6
13.	h5	Qg5
14.	Qf3	Ng8

Black's queen finds space at the cost of retarded development.

15.	Bxf4	Qf6
16.	Nc3	Bc5
17.	Nd5	Qxb2

This takes the queen away from the action. Sometimes called "the poisoned pawn", the b-pawn is frequently put on offer in modern opening play.

| 18. | Bd6 | Qxa1+ |

Position after Black's 18th move

The bishop moves into place for the mating net. Black now accepts the offer of the second rook.

19.	Ke2	Bxg1
20.	e5	Na6
21.	Nxg7+	Kd8
22.	Qf6+	

The final sacrifice.

22.	...	Nxf6
23.	Be7 mate	

190 *A masterpiece of accuracy*

The strategy in this game is clear-cut, White's superiority in space affording greater manoeuvrability for his pieces.

	WHITE	BLACK
	Capablanca	Eliskases
1.	e4	e5
2.	Nf3	Nc6
3.	Bc4	Bc5

The Giuoco Piano is considered a slow game, as its name implies: it is not popular in master play.

4.   Nc3

Another good move here is c3.

4.   ...   Nf6
5.   d3   d6

Decorous development: neither party interferes with the other – yet.

6.   Bg5   h6

This move is important as White was threatening Nd5 followed by an exchange of pieces at f6, when Black would have been compelled to recapture with the pawn, creating serious structural weaknesses.

7.   Bxf6   Qxf6
8.   Nd5   Qd8

To guard against Nxc7+, winning the exchange, and also of course to rescue the queen.

9.   c3

White sacrificed the two bishops (marginally stronger than bishop and knight, remember) but in turn achieved quicker development. The text prepares to press home this advantage.

9.   ...   Ne7
10. Ne3!

The move presents Black with a difficult problem since on 10. ... 0–0; 11. d4, exd4; 12. Nxd4 White would command the centre.

| 10. | ... | **Be6** |

This move is a mistake, as Capablanca demonstrates.

| 11. | **Bxe6** | fxe6 |
| 12. | **Qb3** | |

Threatening two pawns.

12.	...	Qc8
13.	d4	exd4
14.	Nxd4	Bxd4
15.	cxd4	

The first phase may be said to be over. White, by unassuming moves, has gained a distinct advantage in the centre, a well-placed queen (against Black's passive one) and an open c-file for the white rooks.

15.	...	0–0
16.	0–0	Qd7
17.	Rac1	

If 17. Qxb7, Rfb8.

| 17. | ... | Rab8 |

Necessary, since White was now threatening 18. Qxb7, and if 18... Rfb8; 19. Qxc7.

| 18. | Rc3 | d5 |
| 19. | Qc2 | c6 |

Position after White's 15th move

19... Nc6 would have given Black more counter-chances after 20. exd5, exd5; 21. Rc5, Nxd4; 22. Qd3.

20.	e5	Rf4
21.	Qd1	Rbf8
22.	f3	Qd8
23.	g3	R4f7
24.	f4	Nf5
25.	Nxf5	Rxf5
26.	h4	

White has a pawn majority on the king's side whereas Black's queen's side majority has been rendered immobile. White controls more of the board and has a better pawn formation. Small considerations, perhaps, but enough for Capablanca to forge a win.

26.	...	g6
27.	Kg2	Qe7
28.	a3	

White does not wish the black queen to exercise her nuisance value on the queen's wing.

28.	...	Qg7
29.	Rcf3	Qe7
30.	Qc2	Kg7

Black awaits the gathering storm. After 31. g4, White threatened 32. Qxg6+.

31.	g4	R5f7
32.	Kh3	Qd7
33.	b4	Rg8
34.	Rg1	Kh8
35.	Qd2	

Threatening f5.

35.	...	Rh7
36.	Qf2	h5
37.	gxh5	Rxh5

If here 37... gxh5; 38. Rg5, followed by a concentration of pieces on the g-file would be decisive.

38.	Rg5	Qh7
39.	Qg3	Qh6
40.	Qg4	Rg7
41.	Rg3	Kh7

On 41... Rh7; 42. Rxh5, Qxh5; 43. Qxh5, gxh5; 44. Rg6, Re7; 45. Rh6+ would win.

| 42. | Rg2 | |

The object of this move is to bring the rook to the defence of the h-pawn and release the queen for action elsewhere.

| 42. | ... | Kg8 |

43.	Kg3	Kh7
44.	Rh2	Re7

For now White did threaten Qxe6.

45.	Rh3	Kg7

A weak move, but Black's hopes are fading. 45... Re8 was better.

46.	Rxh5	Qxh5
47.	Qxh5	gxh5
48.	f5!	

The break-through.

48.	...	exf5
49.	Kf4	Re6

If 49... Rf7; 50. Rg3 ch., Kh6; 51. Rg5.

50.	Kxf5	Rg6
51.	e6!	Rg4
52.	Ke5	Re4+
53	Kd6	Rxd4
54.	Re3	Resigns

The pawn must go through to queen.

191 *The Inimitable Bobby Fischer*

This game demonstrates the folly of neglecting development and the safety of the king.

	WHITE	BLACK
	Fischer	Geller
1.	e4	e5

2.	Nf3	Nc6
3.	Bb5	a6
4.	Ba4	d6
5.	0–0	Bg4
6.	h3	Bh5

The ingenious sacrifice 6... h5; is quite playable: if 7. hxg4, hxg4 the knight is attacked, and, if it moves, Black will threaten mate by 8... Qh4.

7.	c3	Qf6
8.	g4	

This pawn advance in front of the castled king is usually dangerous; however Fischer has calculated that Black's king's side is uncoordinated.

8.	...	Bg6
9.	d4	Bxe4

White has sacrificed a pawn to open up the game.

10.	Nbd2	Bg6
11.	Bxc6+	bxc6

The black king now has no shelter on the queen's side.

12.	dxe5	dxe5
13.	Nxe5	Bd6

Not 13... Qxe5 because Black would lose his queen after 14. Re1.

14.	Nxg6	Qxg6
15.	Re1+	Kf8
16.	Nc4	h5
17.	Nxd6	cxd6

18.	Bf4	d5?

This move loses quickly. Somewhat better might have been 18... Rd8; 19. Qe2, hxg4; 20. hxg4 and Black is practically in zugszwang.

19.	Qb3	hxg4
20.	Qb7!	gxh3 dis ch
21.	Bg3	Rd8
22.	Qb4+	Resigns

Black must lose knight and rook after 22... Ne7; 23. Qxe7+, Kg8; 24. Qxd8+. See diagram.

Position after Black's 19th move

192 *A World Championship Clash*

An example of a nice-controlled king's-side attack. The players castle on opposite sides which usually makes for an exciting contest.

	WHITE	BLACK
	Karpov	Korchnoi
1.	e4	c5
2.	Nf3	d6
3.	d4	cxd4
4.	Nxd4	Nf6
5.	Nc3	g6
6.	Be3	Bg7
7.	f3	

This is a sharp continuation in which White plans to castle queen's side and attack on the king's side.

7.	...	Nc6
8.	Qd2	0–0
9.	Bc4	Bd7
10.	h4	Rc8
11.	Bb3	Ne5
12.	0–0–0	Nc4
13.	Bxc4	Rxc4
14.	h5	Nxh5

White has given up a pawn to clear the file for the king's rook.

15.	g4	Nf6
16.	Nde2	Qa5
17.	Bh6	

This is a favourite manoeuvre to get rid of a fianchet-toed bishop which here both defends the king and indirectly attacks White's castled position.

17.	...	Bxh6
18.	Qxh6	Rfc8
19.	Rd3	

It is necessary to defend the knight and consolidate the defence before launching the final attack on the king's side. Notice the black knight is tied to the defence of the h-pawn which is under pressure from the white queen and rook.

| 19. | ... | R4c5 |
| 20. | g5 | Rxg5 |

The black rook has been lured from its attacking position on the c-file.

21.	Rd5	Rxd5
22.	Nxd5	Re8
23.	Nef4	Bc6
24.	e5!	Bxd5

If 24... dxe5; 25. Nxf6+, exf6; 26. Nh5.

Position after Black's 23rd move

25.	exf6	exf6
26.	Qxh7+	Kf8
27.	Qh8+	Resigns

After 27... Ke7; 28, Nxd5+, Qxd5; 29. Re1+ and
White wins a rook or a queen for a rook.

193   *The Dynamism of the World's No. 1*

In this game the centre is locked, both sides castle king's
side and seek play on opposite wings. This time it is
Black who attacks on the king's side, and Kasparov
finishes the game with a startling coup-de-grace.

	WHITE Piket	BLACK Kasparov
1.	d4	Nf6
2.	Nf3	g6
3.	c4	Bg7

The 'Indian' bishop is in place. White does not venture
the Four Pawns Attack (see the opening demonstrated in
130) and instead develops circumspectly.

4.	Nc3	0–0
5.	e4	d6
6.	Be2	e5
7.	0–0	Nc6
8.	d5	

Locking the centre.

8.	...	Ne7
9.	Ne1	

In order to mobilise the f-pawn.

9.	...	Nd7
10.	Be3	f5
11.	f3	f4
12.	Bf2	g5

13.   b4

White counter-attacks on the queen's side.

13.	...	Nf6
14.	c5	Ng6
15.	cxd6	

Opening the c-file.

15.	...	cxd6
16.	Rc1	Rf7
17.	a4	Bf8
18.	a5	Bd7
19.	Nb5	g4

If 20. fxg4, the white e-pawn is undefended.

20.	Nc7	g3!
21.	Nxa8	Nh5

Maintaining the pressure. After 21... gxf2+; 22. Rxf2, Qxa8 White gains material but the attack disappears.

Position after Black's 20th move

22.	Kh1

If 22. Bxa7, Qh4; and White cannot survive.

22.	...	gxf2
23.	Rxf2	Ng3+

The knight can't be taken (24. hxg3, fxg3 with Qh4+ to follow).

24.	Kg1	Qxa8
25.	Bc4	

White still dare not take the knight.

25.	...	a6
26.	Qd3	Qa7
27.	b5	axb5
28.	Bxb5	Nh1!
	Resigns	

Black wins rook for knight to secure a bishop-for-pawn advantage. See diagram.

Final position

The best method of defence is often attack, particularly if a win is necessary. Britain is now in the top rank of chess-playing nations, and in this game the British Grandmaster Speelman shows why.

	WHITE Timman	BLACK Speelman
1.	e4	e5
2.	Nf3	Nc6
3.	Bb5	f5

An aggressive, but little-played line. 3... a6, Nf6, or d6 are usual.

4.	Nc3	fxe4
5.	Nxe4	d5
6.	Nxe5	dxe4
7.	Nxc6	Qg5

Early fireworks, but this is a trodden path.

8.	Qe2	Nf6
9.	f4	

Defending the g-pawn. Notice that Black cannot capture *en passant* as Black's e-pawn is pinned.

9.	...	Qxf4
10.	Ne5 dis ch	c6
11.	d4	Qh4+
12.	g3	Qh3
13.	Bc4	

Better than 13. Nxc6.

13.	...	Be6
14.	Bg5	0–0–0
15.	0–0–0	

Both kings fly to safety.

15.	...	Bd6
16.	Nf7	Bxf7
17.	Bxf7	Rhf8
18.	Bc4	Rde8
19.	d5	c5

After this move White's bishop has a bleak future.

20.	Rhf1	Kb8
21.	Bf4	Rd8
22.	Bg5	a6

Preparing an eventual b5.

23.	Bxf6	gxf6
24.	Qxe4	Qxh2
25.	Rh1	Qxg3
26.	Rxh7	Rfe8
27.	Qf5	

This loses. White's only chance was 27. Qh4, Qf4+;
28. Kb1.

27.	...	b5
28.	Bf1	

Otherwise the bishop is lost. If 28. Bb3, c4; and if
instead 28. Bd3, c4; 29. Be4, Qe3+; etc.

28.	...	Re1
29.	Qh5	

Position after Black's 27th move

If 29. Qd3, there follows 29... Bf4+; 30. Kb1, Qxd3 winning.

29.	...	Qf4+
30.	Kb1	Qxf1
	Resigns	

PART NINE

The World of Chess

195 *Where Next?*

Learning to play chess is only the start of your pleasure – and I hope that it has been a pleasure so far. Already you have probably played a few games, your interest has increased and you want to know what other opportunities for play are open to you and what to do next to improve your standard.

Perhaps most chessplayers get all they want out of the game just by playing with friends. After all, life is a full place and one cannot be an expert in everything. However, only a little effort is needed to lift you above this huge group of casual players and there is a lot to be gained. If you are not already a member of a school or other chess club you may wish to join one; it is likely there is one locally. Soon you will have the opportunity for match or tournament play which is more of a challenge than friendly chess or 'skittles' as it is often called. In competitive chess silence during play and 'touch and move' are enforced, and you may also be expected to keep a score of the game (score sheets are provided for matches; you enter each move of both sides as it is played and you are free to use any notation). One point is awarded for a win and half a point for a draw, and the winner is of course the side or player with the most points.

Later you may use a chess clock. This is two ordinary clocks in one unit, one clock recording the time you take for your moves and the other that taken by your opponent for his moves. Only the clock of the player whose turn it is to move is running at any one time. Clocks make sure that neither player sits and thinks (or perhaps just sits!) for too long. A typical rate of play is 24 moves in one hour which, as you are also free to think in your opponent's time, means an average of nearly five minutes for each move – slow enough!

Also, if you make your obvious moves quickly you have more time for those positions in which you need to think longer. A player who oversteps the time limit loses the game. Illustrated are a chess clock and (part of) a score sheet. Note the little 'flags' on the clock. The flag is lifted by the minute hand and drops on the hour to avoid dispute about the exact time taken. The latest chess clocks are digital.

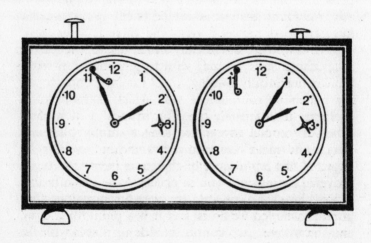

EVENT	CLUB CHAMPIONSHIP				
DATE	19th OCTOBER		ROUND	4	

WHITE	A. Bishop		BLACK	A. Knight	
	WHITE	**BLACK**		**WHITE**	**BLACK**
1	Nf3	Nf6	25	gxh4	Nd3
2	c4	g6	26	a6	Nc5
3	g3	Bg7	27	axb7	Nxb7
4	Nc3	d6	28	dxc6	Resigns
5	d4	0-0	29		
6	Bg2	c6	30	1	0
7	0-0	Nbd7	31		
8	e4	Rb8			
9	a4	Qc			
10					

197 *Unfinished Games*

A match game unfinished when play is stopped is either
adjourned or *adjudicated*.

(a) An *adjourned* game is one which is resumed at
another time;

(b) An *adjudicated* game is one in which the players
cannot agree a result and the position is passed to
an expert for a verdict.

Certain procedures are called for in each of these cases.
In an adjourned game, the player to move at close of
play must write his move down without making the
move on the board or telling his opponent what he has
played. The move is put in an envelope which is then
sealed. You are allowed to study an adjourned position
if you wish (you would be silly if you did not!) and you
may even seek advice on it although some players
consider this unfair. The envelope is not opened until

the game is restarted when the *sealed move*, as it is called, is made on the board. In an adjudicated game, the position at the close showing whose turn it is to move is passed by each player to his match captain with a claim as to the result.

198 *Chess in Britain*

Chess clubs usually meet one or two evenings a week and apart from affording the opportunity for friendly games, offer various activities such as tournaments, matches against other clubs, etc. Most chess clubs are affiliated to their respective County Associations which in turn are affiliated to one or other of the regional Unions. These Unions, together with a few other independent bodies, send delegates to the British Chess Federation which is responsible for organised chess on a national basis.

A pleasing feature of chess life is that the traveller or holiday-maker is likely to find a welcome at the local club whether at home or abroad.

A feature of chess in recent years has been the rise in popularity of the congress. A chess congress is an open tournament (usually a number of tournaments) covering anything from a day to a fortnight. Congresses are often arranged at resorts so that the competitor combines chess with a holiday. Normally one game is played each day, but in one-day and weekend events a fast time-limit, or a time-limit per game, is usual.

199 *Chess Computers*

In recent years the chess computer has become a popular opponent. Technical development in this field has been dramatic, and few players can now match the strength of the more advanced models. A chess computer is an always-ready opponent, capable of playing at a number of different speeds and levels, and usually offering a range of other facilities including advice on the best move, retracting moves, repeating games and solving problems. All computers have built-in opening repertoires. If no human guidance is at hand, a chess computer or software program, preferably the most advanced you can afford, is a recommended purchase.

200 *Correspondence Chess*

Increasingly players are turning to the Internet for their chess. It is alleged that there are half-a-million sites devoted to the game! You can play by e-mail against players of your own strength and even against grandmasters. There is much more: tuition, tournaments, game scores, news coverage, problems, in fact every aspect of the game you can think of. And for those not yet online there are postal chess tournaments in which you can compete with players round the world.

201 *Literature*

Chess is said to have had more books written about it than any other sport or game. This is doubtful, but there is certain to be a good collection in your local Public Library. All modern books use the algebraic notation with which you are now familiar. There are also chess magazines in many languages. The two leading British periodicals, both monthlies, are *The British Chess Magazine* and *Chess Monthly*.

202

Match games are graded in the UK. That is to say, you are given a ranking, indicated by a number, according to who you play against and your results. At the top (a long way to go!) there are titles awarded by The British Chess Federation and the international authority FIDE (Federation Internationale des Echecs).

Index